T0363158

THE ART OF BLEISURE

THE ART OF
BLEISURE

Travel the world, make money
and live a life you love now

EMMA LOVELL

In *The Art of Bleisure* author Emma Lovell is your VIP travel guide to a world of business and personal fulfillment.
ANNA FEATHERSTONE, founder, Bold Authors

Emma is one of the most enthusiastic and positive people I know, and her approach to combining business and leisure—aka Bleisure—is super inspiring. Now she's sharing all she's learned about travel and business in her new book. It's a fantastic read packed full of tips and learning from Emma's diverse career and extensive travels. If you've ever dreamed of swapping your desk for a daypack and seeing the world while you work, this is the book for you.
ANGELA PICKETT, copywriter

Have you been fantasizing about the laptop lifestyle, traveling the world while earning a living? Why not live it? Emma Lovell has coined this way of life Bleisure (seamlessly combining business with leisure) and in her debut book shares how it can be done. Make no mistake, Emma's Bleisurely lifestyle wasn't handed to her on a silver platter and in this part-autobiography, part-how-to-guide she shares her journey—warts and all—to inspire readers ready to create a lifestyle they love on their terms. A masterful storyteller, Emma walks her talk and shows what's possible when someone sets out to chase their dreams with determination. I'm already looking forward to her next book.
SHARI BREWER, founder, Allsorts Copywriting

Emma's enthusiasm and passion shine through this book, much like her in person. It's hard not to be inspired to create a life you love when you hear how she has made it work for her. A practical, thoughtful, and insightful guide to get you started.
LOU ACHESON, marketing manager

Acknowledgement of country

I acknowledge the traditional owners and custodians of the land on which I wrote most of this book, Yugambeh Country. I recognize Aboriginal and Torres Strait Islander peoples as the First Peoples of this place now known as Australia.

I am grateful for the continuing care of the lands, waterways and skies where I work, live, listen, learn and play. From wherever you are reading or listening, I pay my respects to the Elders past and present.

Always was, always will be, Aboriginal land.

For Finn and Mathew, you are my greatest WHY.
You help me focus daily on living a life I love.
Here's to many more adventures ahead my darlings.

First published in 2024 by Emma Lovell

© Emma Lovell 2024
The moral rights of the author have been asserted

All rights reserved. Except as permitted under the *Australian Copyright Act 1968* (for example, a fair dealing for the purposes of study, research, criticism or review), no part of this book may be reproduced, stored in a retrieval system, communicated or transmitted in any form or by any means without prior written permission.

All inquiries should be made to the author.

A catalogue entry for this book is available from the National Library of Australia.

Printed in Australia
Book production and text design by Publish Central
Cover design by Leith Hudson

The paper this book is printed on is certified as environmentally friendly.

Disclaimer

The material in this publication is of the nature of general comment only, and does not represent professional advice. It is not intended to provide specific guidance for particular circumstances and it should not be relied on as the basis for any decision to take action or not take action on any matter which it covers. Readers should obtain professional advice where appropriate, before making any such decision. To the maximum extent permitted by law, the author and publisher disclaim all responsibility and liability to any person, arising directly or indirectly from any person taking or not taking action based on the information in this publication.

CONTENTS

HOW TO USE THIS BOOK

Welcome lovely reader. Delighted to have you here and I can't wait to jump in.

But before we do, a note on how you can best use this book. You do not have to read it cover to cover. Although there is a flow, if you're anything like me, you'll want to flick around and dabble in any order you choose. That's OK. You're busy. That's why I've used lots of bullet points, lists, headings and more to make this a super easy read.

I have structured this book as follows:

- **First third:** my story and journey to the Bleisure life, covering the three main areas of business, travel and self-care.

- **Second third:** how to apply Bleisure to your life, covering income, travel hacks, work hacks and more.

- **Last bit:** how I'm doing Bleisure now, with plenty of inspiration about how you can apply it.

You'll also find:

- **Case studies:** don't take my word for it about the Bleisure life; hear how these incredible people make it work for them.

- **Questions for reflection:** at the end of each chapter, you'll find a series of questions to apply to your own life so you can start building your "Bleisure Life Plan."

- **Short and sweet:** Short on time? This is for you. Skip to the end of each chapter for the summary.

I hope you find this book a helpful resource as you explore what Bleisure looks like in your own life. Now, go forth. Choose your own adventure. I'm excited about what you'll discover.

Emma x

FOREWORD

When Emma Lovell reached out to me and asked me to write the foreword for her book, I'll admit the first thing I did was head to Google and type in the word "Bleisure." As someone who's traveled extensively combining business with pleasure for decades now, I'm embarrassed to say I should have been more familiar with the term.

If you're like me and have chosen to walk the path of entrepreneurship, I take my hat off to you. It's not for the fainthearted. What I know about entrepreneurs is that they're always looking to maximize their time and squeeze as much out of every opportunity as they can. For me, this has meant traveling with my six children—preferably not all at once as I value my sanity and mental health—and it's often meant tacking on a few days with them to enjoy wherever my business needs me to be. Before my son Ryder turned three months old, I had taken him from Australia to New York on three separate trips. He had also taken his first helicopter ride over Uluru as a newborn baby right after a conference I had produced there and visited Necker Island in the Caribbean for the same reason.

Bleisure is not new, and it's on the rise. It's a perk that many employees consider important when choosing where to work, and whether to stay with that employer. A full 86% of Bleisure travelers see this corporate travel perk as a key component to their career development and a crucial factor in cementing key business relationships.

Emma Lovell has taken it upon herself, through years and years of personal research, to become your expert when it comes to mastering Bleisure travel. I've known Emma for a long time now and am always impressed with her enthusiasm. She grasps life and business with both hands. And now she's here to teach us all she knows.

Congratulations Emma on helping educate me on this rising trend and the thousands of others you'll also help with this book. Wishing you nothing but continued success. Now book that business trip, add on a few days just for you (or bring your kids along as well if you're brave).

Emma Isaacs
Founder and Global CEO, Business Chicks
emmaisaacs.com
businesschicks.com

PROLOGUE

Have you ever had your world stop? Everything goes quiet. There's nothing but you and your thoughts. Time freezes. There's stillness. This life-changing moment can go one of two ways. When I had that moment, I heard a voice in my head say, "Please, God. Don't let this be it."

I was sitting in the snow on the side of Australia's tallest mountain, Mount Kosciuszko, at Thredbo ski resort. I'd been competing in the university games representing the University of Technology Sydney for snowboarding and I hit a jump during the competition. Before that jump, I said to myself, "Man up." As I flew, I knew I'd made the wrong decision. I fell over 2 yards and landed on the knuckle of the jump—a hard compacted mound of snow I should have cleared.

When I hit the ground, time froze. I thought, *my life as I know it is over*. There was a real chance I had broken my back and might not walk again. Milliseconds felt like hours. I let out the most blood-curdling primal scream—a sound you wouldn't think possible from a human—but the pain was instant.

People rushed to my aid and called the ski patrol, whose job is to help injured skiers and snowboarders. They took me down the mountain in a kayak-like vehicle, also known as "the blood bin."

On the journey down, I fell silent. I stopped screaming. I knew this was a turning point in my life.

I spent eight days in the hospital. The doctors told me I'd be spending 10 weeks in a back brace. If I didn't rest, they told me, I would have serious health consequences for the rest of my life. I then had another eight months of rehabilitation. During my recovery, I had time and space to think about what I wanted for my life for the first time in quite a while.

What did I want? I wanted freedom. To be in charge. To have control. I wanted to run a business and run my own life. On September 1, 2009, my business Lovelly Communications was born. A dramatic start to a business journey, but I started. And I am still running a profitable business today.

You don't need to take the traditional career path. You, too, can choose your path. You can take an alternate path and have a successful business or career doing what you love the way you want.

That's not to say it's all rainbows and sunshine all the time. I have faced challenges and I will share them. And I will share how I combine business, travel and self-care to live a life I love. Not one day or some day in the future. Not when I retire.

But now.

And I'll show you how you can, too.

INTRODUCTION

The year 2023 began with a thud. Tragedy after tragedy. Lives cut short. My heartache and pain felt like waves crashing over me, again and again.

But through all the challenges and exhaustion that comes with grief, I found opportunity. For example, I felt an urgent need to write this book. Why do we decide to go after our dreams only when other people's lives are cut short?

I have been living a Bleisure life since I started my business in 2009, inspired by the shock of breaking my back in a snowboarding accident (see my prologue). In 2023, having Bleisure incorporated into my life had never felt more crucial.

HOW IT BEGAN

The first tragedy of 2023 happened January 2. In a horrific helicopter crash next to Sea World Australia, four people lost their lives and three others were injured. My husband, Mathew, works at Sea World Australia. The community was in shock and my husband, who worked that day, became a first responder, supporting rescue crews and emergency personnel by ferrying them to and from the crash by boat.

My son and I pulled up at Mathew's work 20 minutes before the chaos erupted. It was all so terribly close to home as the night before I'd had the Sea World Helicopter webpage open to book our own ride. Friends knew of my plans and were messaging to check on us, not knowing how involved Mathew was due to his work role. The reminder that life is short was stark that day.

"Why do we decide to go after our dreams only when other people's lives are cut short?"

The next day, January 3, tragedy struck again. Even closer to home. Everyone in my family had been waiting on my 11-month-old nephew's medical results. Louis' health had been declining and for six long weeks, the doctors couldn't provide any answers.

My brother, James, called me to say that Louis had a rare genetic condition called "white matter disease." One week later, January 10, the doctors gave Louis just one to two years to live. Devastating. Heartbreaking. The news could not possibly have been worse.

HOW 2023 GOT WORSE

On March 24, my brother and his wife visited our Gold Coast home to make precious memories with Louis. It was a beautiful time, but also emotionally and mentally challenging for us all. We tried to savor each moment but kept looking ahead and feeling terrible grief. And I had to overcome my feelings of guilt at having my healthy son, then two-year-old Finn, while they were losing theirs.

The next day, my grandmother died at age 92. Grief piled on top of grief.

There's no grief Olympics. There's no winner for the person who suffers the most. Grief is an undercurrent that runs through my family now and will impact us forever. Sadly, darling Louis died while I was writing this book. Grief has become something we live with, our norm for the foreseeable path ahead.

As I came out of that deep fog and despair of the early part of 2023, I turned a corner. I needed to change my business and my life. I wanted processes in place so I could take a break when I needed it, to visit my family when they needed me, and not hustle and feel the pressure of work. I started making changes.

MORE TO COME

But 2023 wasn't done with me yet. Oh no.

I don't like to label years as good or bad. Every year has ups and downs. But 2023 was a shit show and, to date, the most challenging year of my life.

In August, I got more shocking news. My friend Steph was severely ill. I knew she had battled a brain tumor and breast cancer over the past few years, but she kept coming through. Then I discovered she had days, weeks, or maybe a month to live.

Five days later, I discovered another dear friend, my roommate from a student exchange trip I took to Mexico in 2009, had died of breast cancer. I knew she had cancer. She'd been having treatment, but I hadn't seen the decline. She lived in Germany and I hadn't heard from her recently and the news was a horrible shock. She was 37, just one year older than me. She hadn't had the life she deserved. Although she'd done so many wonderful things, she wanted to live and give so much more.

Two pieces of devastating news in one week. I woke up the next day and, then and there, committed to go after what I wanted. I'd been dreaming of a future home, a place I wanted to live with my son and husband. So, we got in the car and drove out to a beautiful area where we plan to live one day. We patted horses; we visited open homes and we ate at cafes. I soaked it all in, aware of the lack of time to make these dreams a reality and feeling inspired to bring the vision forward.

One week later, my dear friend Steph sadly left this world. I was fortunate to see her in hospital. It was the first time I'd seen someone so close to death. Dealing with death and ways to approach it is not our strong suit here in Australia. I felt privileged to share those precious moments with Steph. I got to tell her I loved her and that she meant so much to me. Her final words to me as I left the room were, "You light up the world." What a gift.

As tragic as it is to lose another beautiful friend, I want to honor Steph for role modeling how to live a good and full life. She and her amazing husband Paul showed me how to be an incredible couple; how parents can be awesome and cool while still doing things for themselves; and how to have a total blast.

As I grappled with all this grief, my kinesiologist gave me a beautiful message. She said, "Grief clarifies living." I wrote it on a sticky note and put it on my wall as a guiding principle for my year.

PRIORITIES

The gift of grief is clarity; what you say you want in your life but are not prioritizing. Prioritizing this book came through loud and clear for me. Yes, I prioritize my home, my travels and my boys, of course. But this book could have become my regret—not sharing this message about the alternate career path you can take. To live a life of Bleisure and to find the harmony between work and life. To live a life you love now.

So many people subscribe to a model of life that goes work, work, work, then play. Or save, save, save, for a day when you go on an incredible journey in retirement. You work hard, so one day you get to live.

But we don't all get that day in the future. None of us knows how long we have. We don't know if we get one year, seven years, 35 years or 100 years. I know it's not possible to live every single day as if it's your last, and nor am I encouraging you to blow all your cash and just live it up tomorrow.

But you can bring your dreams forward. If you had days to live, what would be your one regret? And what would be your legacy? I would deeply regret not having written this book and not having shared my story. I'd regret not having shared this Bleisure philosophy and way of life. I want to pass on stories about my lessons over the years. If nothing else, I will remind myself to keep living my life the way I want.

GRATITUDE

Despite so much tragedy around me, I reminded myself of what I have achieved so far and I'm proud and grateful. I have worked and lived sustainably for a long time. I don't think I'll ever retire as such. I'll just keep creating.

Drawing a line between the working part of your life and the enjoying part is not a fulfilling way to live. Why can't we integrate the activities we love and have pockets of enjoyment throughout our lives? It's about bringing your work and life into alignment to make it work.

It takes work and it's a choice. You may have challenges—believe me, I'll share many—but I know the art of Bleisure can bring freedom and joy.

Running a business might not be for you, but I'm going to share with you many ways that you can bring in income. You can have multiple income streams and not rely upon one job or one business or one client. Work is not the be all and end all. It's a big part of our lives, but I work to live. I don't live to work.

I'll share with you how to do all of this profitably so you are not gallivanting around and burning through your funds (been there, done that). And I'll share how to take care of yourself, too, because you are the top priority and, sorry to be clichéd, but you must put your oxygen mask on first.

I'll be sharing with you what didn't work, when I failed and when it was hard because that's the truth. Even with sacrifices, challenges, and ups and downs, I wouldn't change any of this.

I wouldn't even change breaking my back. Breaking my back helped me start my business, taught me to slow down, to rest, and it led me to where I am today. It's all part of the journey, to be clichéd again.

LUCKILY FOR ME?

You might think, "Oh that's lucky for you." Or "If she can travel that's great for her, but not everyone can."

The voice in your head creates a list of all the reasons you can't run a business or work the way you want and travel the world. It's telling you why you can't have what I have and why it's not possible for you, but possible for others.

But I'm no different from you. Living a life you love is possible for everyone. You may not want to visit 72 countries; you may not even have a business. It might be something you want to do on the side, or a desire to work from anywhere and not just the place that you live.

You might even just want to include a few extra trips a year around your corporate role. Great, the Bleisure life allows you to decide what works for you.

However, I would like to acknowledge the privilege of living in a country like Australia. I am white; I am blonde haired and blue eyed. I am welcomed with no trouble or difficulty when traveling. Some things are easier for me because of my parents, my background, my family status and structure, my religion and so forth. I have tried hard to be open to learning and to acknowledge when I don't understand and what I don't know.

I remain curious and open to questions about my advantages and to being challenged. If you read this and don't see yourself, I hope I can amend that in the future. I hope that no matter your circumstances, you can choose to live a life you love.

Now I'm not saying that you should spend every dollar that you earn. I've invested in property. I plan to make investments and contribute to my future self. I don't condone spending everything you have. I spent many years living the feast-or-famine life. It's not something I wish to continue, nor would I encourage anyone else to try it.

But this idea of working for years to enjoy your life later is redundant. It's tiresome and it's boring, and I don't think it works. It leads to unhappiness. That is not living. A bold statement? You bet. That is what this book is about. Living a life you love. Now. Not one day or some day in the future.

A SNAPSHOT OF BLEISURE

What does living a life I love look like for me? Right now, it looks like:

- Running my business from wherever my phone and my laptop are.
- Taking trips of one day, five days, 30 days, or 90 days or more at any time I choose.
- Having my husband and son along for the ride.

- Being with my family when they need me most, and not having my business fall apart.
- Building an amazing team who can also work from anywhere in the world for my business and create a life that they love of their own.
- Visiting new countries and having new experiences.
- Soaking up the life in the beautiful Gold Coast location that I've chosen to live in and base myself 60% of the time.
- Living a life I love.

Ultimately, it means freedom.

It means choice.

It means that I get to decide what my life looks like.

So, my adventurous and curious friend, within these pages I will share the journey to running a six-figure business from wherever I am: my lounge room, an apartment in India or a balcony in Hawaii.

I'll share what not to do and anecdotes of times where it went horribly wrong. I'll share the times where it went perfectly right. I'll tell you the figures and the finances and what it takes to travel, sometimes four months of the year, while still running a business and being able to work and earn as you go. I will give you my hacks, my tricks, my tips, and share with you about my dreams, desires and goals and what I plan this Bleisure life to look like in years to come.

You'll hear stories of other incredible people who have created a lot of freedom and flexibility in their lives, and who share my passion for travel. From a touring comedian to your typical corporate employee, these people, like me, have made Bleisure work for them. And they're living a life they love.

It's been a joy to dig through the archives of memory, to revisit destinations and experiences that I love. To be reminded of the lessons I have learned hard, sometimes painfully, and to be grateful for the life that I'm living.

I'm the Bleisure Coach.

I'm living a life I love, running my business and traveling the world. This is Bleisure. Combining business and leisure and finding a flow and harmony so that you can work and live happily long into the future.

I'm fiercely passionate about this topic. But note, as with all things, over time I might change. I'm loving this Bleisure life and adapting and learning as I go. You may pick this book up the year I wrote it or five years from now. I may change and adapt how I do some of these things or even how I think, but I'll always share honestly as I learn and grow. Books are written at a point in time, but I hope you'll find other ways to stay connected with me as this Bleisure life evolves for you, too.

Let my book inspire you to see things differently, to do it your way and to live a life YOU love now.

BLEISURE: THE ART OF COMBINING BUSINESS AND TRAVEL

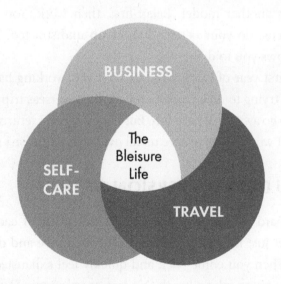

As I sat in the warm bubbling water of the stunning Onsen Hot Pools in Queenstown, New Zealand, I knew I had achieved the Bleisure life I'd been working toward. I gazed out over the breathtaking Shotover River and breathed deeply. I'd made it.

The Business Chicks conference kicked off the next day and I would be there to work—supporting their team, speaking and networking. Making a last-minute change to my flight allowed me to arrive early and relax before the conference. I indulged in a rare moment of me-time. As mum to a toddler and a business owner who's always switched on, this time was bliss. That extra day of relaxing was all I needed.

THIS IS BLEISURE

Business + leisure = Bleisure. I define Bleisure as the ability to integrate travel and leisure into my working life. And I've mastered the art of Bleisure. I no longer subscribe to the work-work-work-then-play model of living. That is the model I learned growing up, and it is the model most of us take for granted. That model says, "I deserve leisure only when I've earned it. Then I can switch off."

There is another model. Relax first, then work. You will find it easier to focus, do your best and show up undistracted. That's what Bleisure allows you to do.

In my first year of business in 2010, I was working hard to repay debts while trying to make money for another overseas trip I'd booked. I planned to go away and have fun. But I knew when I returned, I'd be in more debt. I would have to save up all over again. It wasn't sustainable.

ARE YOU DOING A VERSION OF THIS?

You work hard all year for one big vacation. Out of each 52-week year, you get just four weeks that are all yours to be and do whatever you want. Then you come back and quickly feel exhausted again. Or perhaps you never take a break. No rest or vacations. Maybe you are saving up all your leave for some day—one day in the future.

Well, sadly we don't all get that. None of us knows when our life will be done. You don't have to wait to enjoy your life when you retire … if you're lucky enough to get there.

I'm not here to wait for just four weeks of vacation a year. I've discovered a way for you to include more travel in your life, whether or not you run a business. It's Bleisure. Bleisure is a lifestyle. It's about including travel, rest and recharging often and not waiting for the next vacation.

Simple decisions will boost your energy, build up your reserves and help you live a life you love throughout the year. Like adding an extra night or day at the end of a work trip, as I did in Queenstown. Easy.

HOW I DISCOVERED BLEISURE

I witnessed Bleisure firsthand with my dad. Toward the end of my schooling, Dad was traveling for conferences a few times a year, he was paid to be there; his flights and accommodation covered. And, instead of jetting back home straight away, he'd take some extra time off and relax. He turned a three-day business trip into a seven-day overseas vacation.

I know this worked well because I later worked for the same company, in the public relations and marketing area, and traveled to conferences in places like Japan, Nepal, India, Thailand, Bangladesh and Malaysia. He and I explored these incredible locations after doing our work at the conferences. It was wonderful. I was freelancing for the company, so I had the freedom to determine my work hours. For Dad, as a corporate employee, he made this kind of travel work for him and encouraged his team to do the same.

Could you, no matter your role, take one extra night to stay in a lovely place? Could you refresh and rejuvenate while also doing amazing work?

THE BLEISURE MOVEMENT

The Bleisure movement is coming. Organizations are adapting, introducing well-being programs and allowing employees more flexibility about where and when they work. Some organizations remain resistant, and I see it as my role to educate and change the hearts and minds of their leaders. Bleisure is the way forward. It will increase staff retention. In a LinkedIn post in 2023, Sir Richard Branson, founder of Virgin Airlines, wrote, "Train people well enough so they can leave; treat them well enough so they don't want to."

I provide many examples to follow in this book so you can make Bleisure work for you. The Bleisure lifestyle is possible as an employee—jump to Danielle Phyland's story on page 178 to read more about how. And if you're a business owner, I have case studies for you too.

COVID-19 gave us a gift; "work from anywhere" became a reality. I've worked from anywhere throughout my business journey. Now it's the norm. That has made my work easier because people understand you don't have to be in a physical office to do great work.

NOT A DIGITAL NOMAD

I'm not talking about being a digital nomad. I am not a digital nomad and I'm not a fan of the term. To me, a digital nomad is someone who works and travels for an extended period—months or even years. They work from somewhere like Bali or another tropical location and they do their work online. But they do not work differently. They just work from elsewhere.

The reason I steer clear of the "digital nomad" tag is because I don't want you to think traveling for months at a time and basing yourself out of an island destination abroad is the only way to combine work and travel. Bleisure is about mixing leisure and work daily or at least weekly.

Also, I don't want you to think you can only travel if you work in the digital space. I have done so many types of work over the years. There are so many ways you can make money, as we'll explore in my chapter about diversifying your income streams.

WHY BLEISURE IS FOR ME

No, I did not make the word Bleisure up. According to Wikipedia, Jacob Strand and Myriam Rayman first used the term in 2009. Strand was a future forecaster for the brand agency The Future Laboratory, and Miriam Rayman was a journalist and futurologist.

But I embrace the term and I live it. Bleisure is the way I live my life and have since I started my business in 2009. It might be the future for many, but it's my past, present and future. I just didn't always realize it.

In fact, in 2023, I recognized I was still buying into the old myth: "you can't make money from travel." Although I had successfully made money from travel and during travel over the years, I didn't recognize that I lived and breathed Bleisure. It was during a dinner with a business friend, Liv Muir, who later became my brand strategist, that I finally saw how I had melded my two great passions. We sat in a bustling restaurant in the suburb of Broadbeach on the Gold Coast, sipping cocktails and eating delicious dumplings, sharing our life stories.

I told Liv that a coach had asked me recently, "What do you want to be known for? What do people come to you for?" I realized it was business and travel and said so to Liv. She joined the dots for me.

"I could run a masterclass on retreats," I said.

"That's not a masterclass; that's a program," she said. "This is your specialty. You can help business owners to travel more."

We joked I could be a business, travel and life coach. And that is what I am. But we took it one step further and made it simpler: I'm The Bleisure Coach. Liv helped me see that I have been successfully combining business and travel all along, in a seamless and fun way, and I show other people it's possible, too.

For the first time, like a lightning bolt striking me, I saw how I could integrate travel into my business and bring all my strengths into alignment. I stepped into my personal brand and owned who I was. I changed the business name to Emma Lovell and began coaching and training others in the three pillars of Bleisure: business, travel and self-care.

It was validating to recognize I had been living this Bleisure life all along and that Bleisure was not just a philosophy to me, but the way I operated. While I was away—whether for months or days—my business always continued.

THE FEAST-OR-FAMINE FALLACY

Yes, sometimes I take vacations that are just vacations. I switch off. I certainly do not advocate working nonstop, forever, until eternity. That's where the self-care element comes in. But you don't have to draw such a definite line between where the work stops and the vacation begins.

There's been one vacation where I declared I wasn't working at all. My husband and I went to India in 2017. I stopped the business. I ended the work agreements with all my clients before the trip and had no work planned for our return. But by the end of that three-and-a-half-week trip, I felt really stressed. It never crossed my mind that I could have said to my clients, "I'm going away for a while and I'm off duty." Coming back to nothing instead of pausing the work caused unnecessary drama. Of course, I got more work, but this feast-or-famine rollercoaster is not a great way to live or work.

NOT "ALWAYS ON"

I love how I run the business now. I am not "always on." Elements of my business run without me. That's how I have developed my business and learned how to fully live the Bleisure life. You can include the leisure and fun as you go. It's about bringing together your life interests. Work and play are both important. You can have fun doing your work. But you can also add in more leisure regularly. Find a healthier balance than the annual allocated leave, which even business owners often subscribe to.

Say you have a business event, like a conference, and it finishes on a Friday night. Then first thing Saturday morning, you head home. And obviously if you've got a family or other commitments, sometimes that is necessary. But I know so many people who don't have those commitments. Or they do, but they could just take one more night instead of doing more work, going full force, being on, and even socializing through work. And then you just go straight back to life.

When you're in this beautiful place, why not make the most of it? Sometimes, when you attend conferences and events, you don't even get the chance to enjoy your surroundings. They put you in this fab resort and then make a program and itinerary that's so jam-packed, you barely get to walk around the hotel, let alone rest in your luscious room.

Then it ends and you just leave.

I know I'm really hammering this point home right now, but why don't you just take one or two nights extra? You can even get there early, one day before. Take one day of leave if you're in a full-time job. If you're a business owner like me, take your laptop and just work from there. You're the boss. You decide.

With conferences and events, give yourself time to download what you've learned. You've had your mind expanded, you've met new people, you've made new connections, and then if you don't give yourself time, you don't integrate that information. You just write a bunch of notes, shove them in a drawer, and get on with your life again.

Why are you rushing back to your life? The experience, the trip, the work—it's all part of your life. That's Bleisure. The fusion and harmony of work and life.

MOMENTS I MISSED

There's always more to learn about Bleisure and I'm speaking from experience. I too have missed opportunities to make the most of incredible locations around the world because I rushed back to work. I'm now kicking myself. But I was young.

For example, in 2011 I trekked Mount Kilimanjaro in Tanzania, Africa. The largest freestanding mountain in the world (19,340.55 feet, and I earned every single foot of that milestone. You bet I'm bragging about it). It was a 10-day trip. I had paid thousands of dollars and traveled thousands of miles to get there. It wasn't a work trip. It was a stretch for me to make it happen.

I could have stayed on for two or three extra days and rested in stunning Zanzibar, a beautiful island off Tanzania. I could have even brought my laptop and had one of the most picturesque office locations in the world for a few days. Well that is what the photos of Zanzibar look like. I am yet to go.

Missing that opportunity for Bleisure is one of my few travel regrets. I missed taking that time for myself to enjoy more of a beautiful country. A few hundred dollars more and I could have had time to process the massive milestone of the climb. But at that time I felt like in order to work, even from my laptop, I had to get back home. Instead of making the most of that big journey, I was back to reality within days and walking around staring at people thinking, "What have you done today? I just climbed a mountain." The rush of the climb was over all too soon. I didn't want to do that race back to the grind again. It was not a good feeling.

Lesson: take a little extra time for you now.

I WASN'T ALWAYS THE BLEISURE QUEEN

I haven't always made the most of working on my laptop. When I was traveling on someone else's tab, such as my role as a tour manager for charity challenges, I felt the need to rush back to my office.

I didn't think to ask if I could change my flights and stay on. I could have taken my laptop with me and done an extra couple of days, which is what I do now. I could have worked a few hours a day, and then hung out by the pool or in a funky hotel, soaking up the vibe for another few days. Taking a flight two days later rarely costs more. Yes, you pay for a hotel for a couple of nights—not a lot more.

So, on one trip as a tour manager on a trek through Sapa Valley in Vietnam, I asked the company if I could extend my stay with some of the group and visit Ninh Binh and Halong Bay. I'd longed to visit these areas but hadn't done so on my last two tour managing trips to the country. Not only were they fine with it, but they also covered the costs of the extra time as my Christmas present. I paid nothing extra to stay on.

Lesson: ask and you shall receive.

THE LAND OF THE LONG WEEKEND

What I'm trying to tell you is there are other ways to make Bleisure work for you.

I'm a huge fan of long weekends. Sneaking in one extra day—just one day off to give yourself a three-day break—gives you a refresh through the year. Leave Thursday night to make the most of the time. Bleisure doesn't have to involve a long break. But my goodness a short break can help.

If you tie in some work or business on your mini-break, great. I find work wherever I am. For example, I went to stay with friends at their family's Airbnb and ended up with them paying me to rewrite their listing for them to better advertise and promote the property. My family's long weekend at the snow with our friends and their families became a research trip. Ergo, Bleisure.

A DAY IN THE BLEISURE LIFE

In my definition of Bleisure, it is more than adding a few days to a work trip or bringing the family along while you're working or taking leisure time during the business trip. I create Bleisure on every trip. Here's an example.

In 2023, I went on a work trip to Melbourne with Jade Warne, my colleague, collaborator, client and friend. Our intention was to host a group photoshoot. She's a photographer, and I was coaching clients about personal branding. A great match-up. We had five clients booked for their photoshoot. Instead of arriving on the morning of the shoot and leaving that night, we built Bleisure into our time together over a few days.

The first day, we arrived in Melbourne and visited a few areas where I had clients. We enjoyed a leisurely brunch and swanned around the streets enjoying ourselves. But we were also working. As entrepreneurs, we are always thinking of ideas and brainstorming for one another. We did that all morning. And we are also both content creators. We captured videos and photos of our experience to share later as marketing, promotional or engaging content for our audiences.

That night, we stayed with a friend and colleague of mine, Danielle Phyland, a fellow travel writer. As you may notice, because I mix business and leisure, my clients and colleagues become dear friends. We enjoyed a meal together, all the while discussing our business plans and sharing ideas. In the past, we have collaborated and given each other leads and clients. This networking is such an important part of the entrepreneurial journey.

The next day, we rocked our photoshoot and delivered an amazing experience to our clients. We also then kept the business and leisure combo going by hosting networking drinks. Networking drinks are a typical business activity, but they are also super fun. We are meeting business colleagues and connections, possibly building relationships that could become fruitful in the future, while also having a lot of fun. What's not to love?

I hope you're seeing how Bleisure could be possible for you.

DON'T BE THROWN OFF KILTER

Now don't sit there saying, "Yeah, but Emma, you can do Bleisure because of the type of work you do." I'm sure you can plan with your clients, with your family and with your friends, getting some additional support, so that you can have a bit of extra time for yourself.

Top up your tank with extra time around your business activities. If finances are the issue, stay with a friend, just like I did. Because it's a business trip, it doesn't mean you can't stay with your friends. And of course, financially that's smarter too. Reducing your costs means you maximize your profit if you are in business like me.

I remember a woman telling me I should stay in hotels on work trips. I met her while networking and connected with her online, as you do. Some people feel they know better than you and feel entitled to give you advice about your life. She attended one of my workshops.

Afterward, she explained she stayed in hotels on her work trips and said, "You really need your own space to work."

At the time, I was traveling a lot between Melbourne and Sydney for a contract with World Vision Australia. She got in my head and made me feel I wasn't a serious and professional businesswoman unless I stayed in a hotel and not with friends.

I booked myself an Airbnb in Melbourne near my friend's house. I spent my mornings with a colleague from work, and my evenings going back and forth to my friend's house. At the office one day, my colleague asked me, "What are you doing tonight?"

I replied, "Having dinner with a friend."

She said, "That's nice."

And I thought, *yes that is nice*.

Why would I come all the way to Melbourne, go to work and go "home" to a hotel each night? What a boring visit and existence. If I'm away from home, from Mathew, why not make it fun and spend time with my gorgeous friend? That night, my friend pointed out that I'd got an Airbnb and ended up at their house each night, anyway. I said I didn't want to overstay my welcome, as my work visits were frequent, and we had jokingly called me the honorary housemate. She responded, "If you ever overstay, I'll let you know. Until then, my house is yours and you're always welcome."

I'd let the silly business versus leisure divisiveness get into my head. The "work can't be fun" trope. Leisure and business must be separated and never shall the twain mix. Staying with friends worked for me. I was rocking the Bleisure life.

Others might tell you that you can't work and live this way, fluidly intertwining your travel, leisure and business. But I am and you can too. Remember, I'm talking about a day or two. I'm not telling you to take a week or 10 days or three weeks. I'm saying start with one extra night, half a day, a morning, two nights if you can. It's not a huge amount, but that bit of loveliness tops up your tank and gives you the energy to keep going.

Stay inspired, motivated and moving toward your dreams with a little Bleisure. Then you don't have to wait for a four-week grand vacation each year. I don't subscribe to it. And I don't think you have to, either.

Have I convinced you that Bleisure is possible yet? Don't worry, we've got another 14 chapters to get to that.

YOU CAN'T: THE MOST MOTIVATING STATEMENT IN THE WORLD

"You can't."

"Really? Just watch me."

Is there anything more motivating? Well, not always. That kind of discouragement can be bloody disheartening and soul crushing. When sharing the idea for this section of the book with a friend, she remarked in horror, "Do people actually say those things to you?"

Yes. This is a list of the really discouraging comments people have made to me over the years. I may have laughed them off or smiled and nodded. Or I fought back and tried to justify or defend myself. Later, I went into a self-doubt spiral.

Can I do it?

Do I need a "real" job?

Is this really a way of life?

Am I being unreasonable?

Can I really make these dreams a reality?

Oh, how I wish I could go back and be a little Emma on my younger self's shoulder. I'd gently whisper words of encouragement in her ear as she faced these remarks. Even now, I still get them. You'll see below, there were even some about this book.

I interviewed my dear friend, Yemi Penn, for this book. I call her "sis," and you can read about her on page 224. As I interviewed her, she said, "Hey, the way you're talking sounds like a justification."

I said, "You're right. It is a justification." This entire book is a justification to my younger self. I said I would, I did and I can do it again.

In 2005, as I sat at a pizza restaurant with high school girlfriends, a farewell party for my big gap year, one friend sidled up to me and said, "You talked about doing these travels in our classes together and I honestly didn't believe you would do it. I thought it was just talk. But you're doing it. Go you."

That was lovely … and kind of rude. There was never any doubt in my mind that the dream I set for myself at nine years old—to travel the world—would become a reality. I laughed and smiled, but it stung me.

I'm sorry to tell you this: people will doubt you, challenge you, question you and even discourage you from the Bleisure life. Choosing to live a life you love takes courage, determination and persistence. So much persistence.

I could have stopped. Any of these statements could have thrown me off course. Some of them have been said to me many, many times. So, let's get these doubts out of your head and onto the paper. Here are a bunch, but you may have some to add. Make your own list. Better to put them on paper than have them swirling around your head and sending you into a self-doubt spiral.

The doubters' favorites

- You can't make money from travel.
- You're not really going to travel around the world for a year?
- How are you going to do it?
- When will you get a job with security?
- You can't keep doing this forever.
- Oh, so you've really got the travel bug, haven't you?
- So, who's paying for this trip?
- Oh wow, with all the travel you do, Dad's credit card must be getting a workout.
- But how can you travel so much?
- Are you profitable?
- You can't make money from travel writing.
- It's very hard to get into travel writing.

- Only very few people succeed in travel writing.
- You don't make much money in the travel industry.
- Travel is dead.
- Social media is dead.
- Copywriting is dead.
- You can't just keep traveling forever.
- Oh well, now you've bought a house, you'll have to slow down the travel.
- Oh well, now you're a mum, the travel's going to stop.
- How do you get your work done when you work from home?
- But how do your clients know you're working when you're not with them?
- You're not really running a business; you're contracting.
- You can't write a book about business and travel; what category would it go in?
- You'll have to slow down when Finn goes to school.
- What does your husband think of all this travel?
- If you're traveling alone, what's happening with your son?

Now, there's a lot there. How are you feeling? It's gross, hey. This suite of messages comes from other people. But they are also thoughts in my head. I have to battle self-doubt. This negativity doesn't help.

Let's shake it off now. Stand up. Deep breath: in and out. Three times. Shift the energy.

My favorite response to the doubters

Now, here are my all-time favorite responses I wish I'd quipped back in the past and probably would say today. Some are smartass and funny; some are practical and true.

I'd love you to write a response to every comment, statement, challenge or doubt that's come up for you. Build your list of awesome responses to take into your own epic life.

Doubter: *You can't make money from travel.*

Me: *I can and I have.*

Doubter: *You're not really going to travel around the world for a year.*

Me: *Yes, I am.*

Doubter: *How are you going to do it?*

Me: *I don't know, yet. But I'm going to give it a red-hot go and figure it out. I'll report back.*

Doubter: *When will you get a job with security?*

Me: *You mean a job where I'm reliant upon one employer's salary, and if they choose to take that job away, I'm left with nothing. You're right, I need a secure job like that.*

Doubter: *You can't keep doing this forever.*

Me: *Why not?*

Doubter: *Oh, so you've really got the travel bug, haven't you?*

Me: *I'm not sick. I enjoy traveling.*

Doubter: *So, who's paying for this trip?*

Me: *Someone, I hope. It's expensive.*

Doubter: *Oh wow, with all the travel you do, Dad's credit card must be getting a workout.*

Me: *Lucky it's platinum then, hey.*

(I didn't joke or reply when an older woman said this to me. Thankfully, both my uncle and Dad jumped in and said, "She pays for it herself." Makes me cry thinking about it. It meant a lot for them to defend me. I didn't have to be rude or disrespectful, or take it on the chin, because they believed in me and backed me.)

Doubter: *But how can you travel so much?*

Me: *Well, first I buy a ticket. Then I board the plane. When I arrive, I call a cab …*

Doubter: *Are you profitable?*

Me: *None of your bee's wax.*

Or

Me: *No. Oh goodness, I best start working on that. Paying to run my business is really going to add up, isn't it?*

Doubter: *You can't make money from travel writing.*

Me: *I can. And I did.*

Doubter: *It's very hard to get into travel writing.*

Me: *Maybe so, but I did it.*

Doubter: *Only very few people succeed in travel writing.*

Me: *Well, I am.*

Doubter: *You don't make much money in the travel industry.*

Me: *I made $12,000 in commissions in one year as a travel representative. This was just one of my side businesses.*

Doubter: *Oh well now you've bought a house, no more travel.*

Me: *I bought it as a long-term investment, so I will travel with more peace of mind now. I have an asset working for me.*

Or

Me: *I shall live in airport lounges now I am a frequent flyer and rent the house out to fund my travels. Huzzah.*

Doubter: *Oh well, now you're a mum, the travel's going to stop.*

Me: *Children under two are free. My travel is just getting started.*

You get the point. I have an answer to every question. If you really want to annoy the doubters, just answer, "Yes, I can" every time. When you choose to live a life by design, there are always going to be challengers and naysayers.

But what they're saying is THEY can't. Or, more accurately, they WON'T.

I know people don't realize their comments can hurt and knock someone off course. They don't realize they are projecting their fears onto you.

And if you have ever said something like these comments, may this act as a reminder to be kind. Always choose kindness first. Even if you have their best interests at heart. When someone is doing something new or challenging, they're already battling doubts. So, even though you're worried, scared, or believe they can't or won't do it, pause and try to be kind first.

These comments may have slowed me from arriving at this destination in my business—a place where my passions align and I know I can serve and help more people. Such comments have made me a little spiteful or resentful at times. I might have gone at my goals like a bull in a China shop just to prove others wrong. But kindness, support and encouragement are as good a motivator as challenges and doubt.

Bleisure takes a certain amount of backing yourself. You choose yourself over security; you follow what you want and what you desire. And sometimes, people will not like you doing that. You can't please everyone. If you ever doubt whether you can change your own life, to increase your Bleisure, refer to this section and the notes you've written for yourself.

Because you can do it.

Dream big, my lovely. And choose your cheerleaders wisely; the ones who are excited, motivated and inspired by your action. They are your champions in this Bleisure life. And remember, I am here for you, cheering you on from wherever I may be working and traveling that week.

Questions for reflection

Note: the way to get the most out of these exercises at the end of each chapter is to write the answers. It will become your Bleisure Life Action Plan, so grab your journal, set the timer and get writing. I like to put a timer on for five to 10 minutes with some instrumental music and just write, write, write.

1. How are you already including Bleisure in your life without recognizing it?

2. How are you finding ways to mix business and leisure?

3. How many weeks of vacation will you be taking this year?

4. How can you take just one more vacation or weekend away or day off this year?

5. Write three places you'd love to visit.

6. Write three friends you'd love to travel with.

7. Write three business events you can attend to contribute to your work or learning that are also somewhere fabulous you want to visit.

8. Work out how much each activity will cost.

Great. Now you have a Bleisure vision board or list at least. This is the first step in creating your Bleisure life—dreaming it.

Short and sweet

- Bleisure combines work/business and leisure.

- You don't have to work, work, work and play.

- You can run your business continuously while including travel and not subscribing to the feast-or-famine way of doing business or travel for that matter.

- You can still take vacations. It doesn't always have to be Bleisure.

- Get excited. Your Bleisure life is about to begin.

2

BROKE MY BACK;
STARTED A BUSINESS

So, how does one go from a broken back to a business?

When lying in a back brace for 10 weeks, there's only so much Sudoku one can do. I had stopped all the work, the study and the partying. I had a great excuse not to socialize as it was excruciating to move. For once, I wasn't going a hundred miles a minute. I found I came to enjoy having less on my agenda. I kept up two subjects at university, but having time to be still gave me the opportunity to think about what I wanted for my future. I had time and space to set up the business I had thought could be something in my future. Why not now? Why not just start?

And I started.

JUST START

It can be as simple as that. Just start a business. I had the Australian Business Number (ABN) for the promotions contracts I did throughout my university years. I registered my business name, Lovelly Communications. I told people "I'm running a business" and that was it.

I'm sure you're thinking there is more to starting a business than that. Like having skills and getting clients and all the other things that might go with a business. And yes, I have skills. I was studying for a Bachelor of Business, majoring in marketing and public relations (PR). But I just started and I learned as I went. And I still run that business today—15 years on.

I've always loved business and known that I'd have a path in it. But it started well before university ... let's take this journey back to where little entrepreneurial Emma began.

YOUNG ENTREPRENEURIAL EMMA

I was nine years old. You think I'm joking, but many entrepreneurs start young. My parents nurtured my entrepreneurial spirit from a young age. For example, I masterminded a garage sale and got the whole family involved. I decided what would be for sale and I was the salesperson on the day. I had "planning meetings" with my parents in the family hot tub. I told them how we could maximize our revenue (not the words I used then, of course) by selling drinks and cupcakes that would keep the customers there longer. I helped Mum and Dad put the ad in the paper and was at the front door with them at 7 a.m. when "keen beans" arrived to buy my Barbie dolls. I loved making money from selling possessions we no longer needed. There's a treasure trove in your home, too.

I decided I could also make money from my skills. I set up a massage business (just with Mum and Dad. Relax). I charged 20 cents for a shoulder, head or back massage. Then I increased the price to 50 cents. Dad sat me down for a discussion on our balcony, outlining the effects of inflation and how my price hike might not be a great business decision. But he graciously accepted the price increase.

I earned a whole $5 from my massage business and I can still picture the ruler-lined spreadsheet I made to track my income. I was proud of the money I earned and I wanted more of it. In the following years, until I was old enough to get a job, I found many ways to bring in extra income.

My parents gave me a small allowance for doing my chores, but I earned more. This included car washing and babysitting for the neighbors. I even helped Mum and Dad at a world congress event for the freight industry they worked in, stuffing goodie bags for all the guests. I tried to get involved in any business activities I could, even reading Dad's work documents. I knew business was in my future.

THE WONDERS OF A JOB

As soon as I was old enough to get a job—14 years and nine months—I was delighted to win my first role at the retailer, Pretzel World. I still remember walking around the shopping center with my resume and my first chat with the manager. I could not wait to get started.

After six months in that job, a family friend mentioned an office junior position. I knew my true calling was in a business setting. I resigned and took the office job. While at high school, my mission became to earn as much as possible. Why? I had set a goal when I was nine years old—that formative age for me. I declared I would take a gap year between school and university to travel the world. I got the atlas out and started planning it. I'd start in the United Kingdom, spend time with my relatives there and then travel to as many places as possible.

I planned this trip for nine years—a long time for a kid. I didn't know how much I needed; just as much as possible. Then I could earn more while living in the U.K. I took on jobs at the office, netball coaching, netball umpiring, waiting on tables at a Tex-Mex restaurant, serving scoops at Cold Rock Ice Creamery and picking up dog poop at a boarding kennel. At one point, I worked three jobs while still at high school.

I saved up $7000—a lot of money when I think about it—over and above my expenses. Those expenses included a $2500 cruise with my final year school mates, socializing, nonessential clothing (such as a sequin skirt), petrol for my car and my phone bill. I'm proud of Emma back then and making that dream come true.

A GAP YEAR TO REMEMBER

In 2006, it was time for my gap year. I planned to be an au pair for my young cousins in England. I stopped over in India on the way. I'd been there the year before with Dad for a conference and fallen in love with the land and its people. I stayed with a colleague and his family. He offered me a sales job at his freight forwarding company's London office. I said I'd think about it.

Once I arrived in England, I quickly realized I was not cut out to be a nanny. Business was my calling. I accepted the role my colleague offered me while in India.

Did I know about sales? *No.*

Had I held a marketing role yet? *No.*

But I studied business in school and my family worked in logistics. I'd figure it out. I stayed for four months and learnt a lot, but realized I was after the gap-year lifestyle. I'd met a bunch of backpackers from Australia and joined them doing the London thing. I was 19 and could try different things. A friend back home hooked me up with a recruitment agency and I landed a role at Gumtree, which was bought by eBay. So, there I was working in eBay's London office.

I thrived in customer service. The managers offered me the chance to rise through the ranks. I could see the possibilities. I could have stayed. But my Bachelor of Business awaited me at the University of Technology Sydney (UTS). I could only defer for one year. It was a sliding doors moment, but I wanted to have a degree, the marketing foundations and not just work my way up.

BACK HOME

In 2007, I returned to Australia and started my degree. I had planned to do another course that allowed a year abroad in Spain. But I learned I could have the experience of living and studying abroad in my course. Sold. It worked out well. I got a scholarship to attend El Tec de Monterrey, Mexico's premier university.

At university, I did a lot of promotions work for telecommunications brands, alcohol companies, major concerts and much more.

This work was flexible and paid very well. And it confirmed my love of promotions and PR.

During my time at university, I worked in the UTS union team organizing student events and helping students with information. They quickly recognized my talent for emceeing and I got a gig hosting the regular lunchtime events and larger concerts on campus.

I LIKE WORK

So, you're getting the memo. I like to work. I like to make money. And I do it in a wide variety of ways. I'm not afraid to work and I'm willing to give things a go to improve my opportunities and my income.

In my first year of university, I worked as an office junior for the freight forwarding industry association my dad led as CEO. I later won a marketing and PR role there as I completed subjects in my business degree.

My family has always been in the freight industry. At one point, my mother, brother, sister, father and I all worked in the industry. Mum and Dad even worked together at the association at one point. This little-known industry moves goods around the world. I love the international nature of it. Through this work, I have created a rich tapestry of connections all over the world. My parents taught me that, while it is important to know your stuff and be good at what you do, it's not what you know, it's who you know. I have always been good at networking, which helped me in my business over the years. I'll share more on how you can maximize this too in Chapter 9: Work hacks.

STOP AND START AGAIN

Then we get to 2009. As you now know, this was the year I broke my back. It was the first time in seven years I'd stopped working. I realized I had a lot of business experience. I had already been operating as a freelancer, I was a one-person business. So, as I recovered from my injury, I registered a business name, started a Twitter (now X) account and told people "I am running a business."

My business name was easy to come up with. I am "Lovell" by name and lovely by nature, so I started calling myself "Lovelly" in school. I did a personal branding workshop and realized I already knew my brand. Then one attendee took it a step further for me. She asked, "Why not double the L" to connect to my surname? Someone else chimed in, "Double L means double the life." Yes, I loved that—Lovelly is double the life and it suited me. So, Lovelly Communications it was.

I tattooed the word on my foot. Then I asked a friend in design studies to take a photo of my tattoo on my foot and turn it into a logo. I still use the logo today. That was now 15 years ago and I am still in business today. I offer new services. I have changed the business—it's now Emma Lovell—but it is the same business.

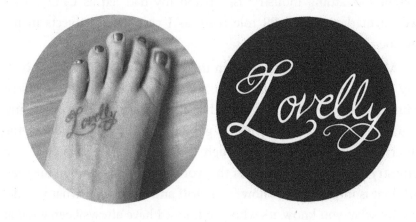

WIN YOUR FIRST CLIENT

So, how does one get their first client? While working with the freight association, I turned that role into my first client. I asked, "Can I invoice you instead of you paying me as an employee?" The answer was, "Yes." Voila. I was a business owner with a client.

My advice for starting a business—just start. As you can see from my experience, you pick up skills and knowledge as you work. That helps you when you start your business. You may not always recognize these skills as applicable to business, but I think if you wrote down all you're capable of, you would find many.

About 20% of new businesses in Australia fail in their first year. Up to 60% of businesses will not survive beyond five years, according to the ASBFEO (Australian Small Business and Family Ombudsman). I'm proud of the longevity I've had.

Over the years, I've had clients across a broad range of industries. I've taken on contracts. I've been a tour manager overseas. I've done freelance writing and much more. I started with PR services and marketing and then social media became a thing. It seems strange now in 2024 to think of a time when social media wasn't a role. Back then it was called playing on Facebook. I was good at it and a company in the travel sector recognized my experience with blogging and socials. They became my client and social media became another service I offered.

A MOVE TO MELBOURNE

In 2011, I moved to Melbourne with a couple of hundred dollars in my pocket and a large personal loan looming over my head. I had little momentum in my business, just a few social media clients. I needed a change. I lived with a friend to find my feet and give it a go. I met her aunt who ran a cleaning business and for the first few weeks of living there that's how I got by. I loved finding and making money anywhere. I quickly established myself as the go-to promo girl in Melbourne and picked up sub-contracting work in copywriting—a new arm to my business.

My copywriting service took off, as did the business. Melbourne is a community city—small communities where you can connect and network quickly. I tapped into the travel and writing communities. Travel Massive was a great one, founded by Ian Cummings. Here I met Theresa Winters, who gave me the opportunity to speak to the UTS alumni about my alternative career path—a talk that built the foundation of this book. It's amazing how people pop into your life at the right time.

‘Are you keeping up?’

I joined the Melbourne Writers Group, hosted by Sandy Sieger. I met future clients, people I sub-contracted to and met a business hero of mine, writer Valerie Khoo. You'll learn more about her in the case study on page 76. I don't fawn over celebrities, but people who have nailed it in business are my superstars. Valerie writes about meeting rock star Jon Bon Jovi for a story as a career highlight. She is my Bon Jovi. Melbourne was my place to shine. My business thrived there.

It's hard to cover off all the work I've done, but here's a quick glimpse of some clients and projects I've had:

- Flight Centre Australia.
- Social media and blogging for Travel Candy.
- Tour manager, fundraising and training support for Soulful Concepts.
- Promoting musicians, including Canadian singer songwriter Charlie A'Court.
- Working with comedians at the Melbourne International Comedy Festival and others, including the popular and talented Bev Killick.
- Emceeing outside the Melbourne Cricket Ground at a football game for a team's major sponsor, car brand Hyundai.

MULTIPLE BUSINESSES

I have created more than one business over the years. When working in the music and comedy industry, I teamed up with another publicist and an agent. We created a company called TLC Publicity (Trio, Lovelly and Corbett). We offered PR and social media packages to touring artists. I went to Canadian Music Week with our Australian artist, Marta Pacek. I worked at a Sydney blues festival, supporting its social media campaign. It was a super fun time and I met amazing people. But we later dissolved that business to focus on our own specialties and projects.

A few years later, I started a pet sitting business.

Are you keeping up?

I ran that business for four years, servicing four states and one international client. I did some pet sitting myself, but I also acted as an agency for about 20 sitters. I loved that business. It was always in the black. It subsidized my lifestyle and paid for an entire trip to Fiji, amongst other things.

While running that business, I saved so much on living costs as I was living in my clients' homes—paying no rent, no electricity, no water and even getting food included sometimes. All my income from pet sitting and from my communications business went into the bank. I saved $42,000 in a matter of six months, which became a deposit to purchase an investment property in Hervey Bay, Queensland. This is a milestone in my life I am extremely proud of.

My contract with World Vision Australia helped me to secure the mortgage for my investment property. Buying a house as a business owner is challenging and a six-month full-time contract helped the bank agree to my mortgage. I loved the work with World Vision. Initially, I took a contract for the 40-Hour Famine 40th anniversary in 2015. They then offered me a full-time contract. Each time a contract ended, I'd go away for a few months and then they would call me back in. I loved it.

Working in the PR and media team for World Vision was a dream come true. I had sponsored a child since I was 17 and loved their work. In 2014, I traveled to Cambodia with them as a tour manager for a team of 18 people who raised more than $84,000 for the charity.

The other fabulous thing about working at World Vision was the contacts. The organization had 400 employees in their Melbourne office and I worked alongside many amazing people doing important work all over the world. World Vision has offices in 92 countries around the world. One day, I spoke with staff in Tanzania, Sri Lanka, Philippines and Canada. It was a dream for this traveler's giving heart.

TRANSFERABLE SKILLS

My foundational communications skills developed during my PR subjects allow me to dip back into that type of work and adapt to different organizations. I secured a contract with the Cure Brain Cancer Foundation in 2018, another lovely way to give back and find some much-needed, consistent income.

I continued my business, contracting, hosting workshops, doing promo work, pet sitting, sub-contracting and finding other ways to earn money.

Over eight years, for example, I subcontracted to two travel companies, helping clients to join trips, fundraise and train for adventures such as cycling in Cambodia or trekking to Mount Kilimanjaro in Tanzania, Machu Picchu in Peru, the Tiger's Nest in Bhutan or to Everest Base Camp—all of which I have done. Participants in these "charity challenges" raise funds for the organization in the lead-up to the adventure. I personally have raised more than $25,000 for charities doing these challenges and the teams I led raised over $500,000. It's rewarding work and it was a steady contract over the years. I just needed my phone and laptop to log in to the system and contact participants.

WRITING AS HOME BASE

If you ask me my job description, it is "writer." Writers are the people I feel at home around. I always keep travel writing alive. I've had my blog, "Lovelly Travels," since I started. The blog gave me a great portfolio and base for writing. I've written articles for Virgin Australia, *The Australian*, Unearth Women and She Defined, to name a few.

I can write from anywhere at any time. Whether I write under my name or as a copywriter, I can take my skill with words and spin it into an income. It's saved me many times in my business and now I love writing for myself and for my audience. And hey, now I'm writing this book!

A WHOLE NEW LEVEL

In 2017, I partnered with an Indian travel company, then called Take Me to India and now called Indus Bound. I'm their Australian representative. I help clients to plan their trips. When I started, I'd been to

India nine times (now 15 times). I connected with this travel company through a travel agent. I didn't think I needed a travel company to do my itinerary. But I sent a few ideas and he came back with such an amazing itinerary that I had to say, "Yes." When we met, he asked me about representing them. The opportunity was too good to ignore. I could talk about my favorite country in the world, get some travel experiences for free and earn a commission. I now partner with Indus Bound for my retreats and help others to plan theirs too.

I was in India again in 2019, though, when I had another life-changing moment—the realization I was over this hustle.

A 10-YEAR RETHINK

I was approaching the 10-year mark of my business and I had had enough. I needed a break, but not just a vacation or a rest. I needed to rethink my entire way of working and operating. This wasn't sustainable for another 10 years and I could see burnout was imminent. I started working with a business coach, completely shifting my direction. I wanted to bring together my skills from the past 10 years. I combined my PR, marketing, social media and copywriting skills to offer personal brand coaching.

I began working with clients who wanted to build their brand and stand out in the marketplace. I was doing what I loved in a new way and I had stepped into the coaching role. When I looked back on my work as a tour manager, the support I'd given teams while contracting and the guidance I offered through my social media workshops, I had been coaching all along. It took me a little while to accept the title of "coach." Some coaches are cowboys. But coaching is what I did and that resonated with people.

This shift occurred just before the COVID-19 pandemic hit. I timed it well. Many of us rethought our lives through the pandemic and people came to me with questions, such as, "Who am I?" "What am I doing with my life?" "How do I define myself without the anchors of a location, a job, a title, a role." Through online networking, my business grew. I cast my net much wider in this virtual space than by attending events.

And then I changed it all again.

ALIGNED TO MY TRUE SELF

I evolved my coaching business to become a business, travel and life coach—communicated more easily as the Bleisure Coach. After teaching people for four years about personal brand, I became a personal brand. I stopped working under my business name, Lovelly Communications, and I rebranded as Emma Lovell. As a coach, speaker and writer, I can do what I love every day. And I do it while pursuing my greatest passion … travel. And as you've probably seen throughout this chapter that's a consistent part of my journey. I'll dive much deeper into this topic next chapter.

YOUR WEALTH OF WORK EXPERIENCE

What has all this got to do with you? You may not run a business yet, but like me, I'm sure you have a wealth of work experience. It amazes me how often my work and life experiences come together at points to create new opportunities. You can do this, too.

It also gives you a bit of context into the breadth and depth of my work over the years and my work ethic. The Bleisure Life didn't just happen, it was a choice and it continues to be. You'll learn more about how I made my income and you can too, in Chapter 5. And you'll learn about the choices in Chapter 7.

But for now, it's over to you.

Questions for reflection

Here are questions for you to explore. I encourage you to write the answers. Pen and paper are the best. Writing on paper is a cathartic exercise and helps you to process better. We'll do these at the end of each chapter so you'll get the hang of it soon. OK go.

1. What was your first ever job?
2. Did you do jobs for money as a kid? What were they and do you remember how much you would make?
3. What was the first thing you ever saved up to buy for yourself?
4. Have you ever had a big financial goal, especially as a kid?
5. Was it to travel the world like me or buy your first car?
6. What roles have you had, paid or not, in your life and career? Write them all down.
7. What are the skills and services you could offer for work? Include cleaning and picking up dog poo. Hey that's how I started a new business.
8. What work have you loved?
9. What work didn't you love and why?
10. If you could do any job/work in the world, what would it be?

Great. Now you have a short version of your own work and life story. You might have even identified some new opportunities to combine some of your skills or to bring back some of the work you once loved.

Short and sweet

- I like to work a lot. And I'm not afraid of working.

- My work and life experiences create business opportunities for me.

- You have more work experience than you realize. Go right back to the beginning of your journey.

- You don't have to be just one thing. What you study or start your career in doesn't have to be where you land.

- Trying out new roles is never a bad experience, just a lesson.

- Just start.

- You can change your mind.

- You can make choices and decide what your work path looks like.

LINDY ALEXANDER
The writer with the dream job

When I thought of including case studies in this book, my mind immediately went to Lindy Alexander. Lindy is an award-winning freelance travel writer who regularly contributes to some of Australia's best-loved publications, such as *The Age*, the *Sydney Morning Herald*, *The Herald-Sun*, *The Australian* and *delicious.* magazine.

There's almost nothing Lindy wouldn't do for a story. During her travels, she has written articles about meditating with monks in Chiang Mai, sleeping in a castle in Jaipur, exploring the floating villages of Bangkok by bike and "heli-hiking" in the Canadian Rockies.

Lindy is also the founder of The Freelancer's Year, a popular blog and online writing course hub for aspiring and established freelance writers.

After following Lindy online for years and marveling at not only her dream job, but the wisdom she shared, we finally met. Lindy was every bit as generous and knowledgeable in person as she was online. She's also a humble, down-to-earth person. For someone who has one of the coolest jobs in the world, Lindy keeps it very real and authentic.

Can you describe your business?

I'm what you could call a "slashie." I have multiple jobs. I'm a freelance writer specializing in food and travel. Additionally, I run an online business offering courses, resources and programs specifically aimed at supporting both aspiring and established freelance writers.

How long have you been working this way?

I wasn't always a freelance writer; I was a social worker for 10 years. I started freelancing in 2012 as a side hustle and I gradually transitioned to full-time by 2017.

I've always felt like a writer but never thought about monetizing it because I could only ever see two pathways—journalism and novel writing. Neither of those appealed to me.

Then when I was in my mid-20s I spent eight months volunteering in rural Uganda. Once a month, I would send an email to family and friends to let them know that I was alive and what was happening. People would write back and say to me, "You should write a book; these emails are so beautiful."

That was the very start of me thinking "I love doing this. I love having these unique experiences and then telling stories about them."

How did you begin with writing and then transition to travel writing?

At the start, I wrote about health, social work and parenting, because that was the space I worked in. Travel writing was still a bit of a dream because I didn't know how I could make it happen. It seemed like something other people could do. I would see photos from writers on these incredible trips and it seemed like they had something special about them that I didn't have.

It was the transition to full-time freelance writing that allowed me to pursue travel writing more seriously.

In your experience, what are the processes involved in being successful in travel writing?

It involves a strategic approach. From understanding a publication to checking if they've recently covered a story you're pitching—it's about the basics. Often, knowing the background processes like a publication's budget or advertiser influences can also affect whether your pitches are accepted.

What are some of the challenges you face with travel writing, but also in living a Bleisure life?

Travel writing isn't always as glamorous as it seems and has its challenges. There are deadlines to meet and stories to craft, often under tight schedules. You're also often trying to meet high expectations. But experiencing new cultures and the stories that come out of it are incredibly rewarding.

Like me, you sometimes enjoy having your family accompany you on trips. Can you share how this impacts your work-life balance?

Being able to include my family in travel assignments brings me immense joy. It adds a layer of enjoyment and makes the experience richer for all of us. It also helps balance my work with pleasure, especially when we can share experiences like exploring new destinations together.

I was recently in Noosa and it was one of the best trips I've taken because my partner and our kids came too. I was working for one of the days where I did a helicopter tour of K'gari (Fraser Island), but the rest of the time, we were in this incredible beachfront apartment and I really blended business, work, travel—everything. It felt so balanced.

My children don't often get to see what I do. I can point to articles that are published but for them to come on a trip helps them to experience it. They may have a very skewed understanding of my work when they see me literally flying in a helicopter past our apartment. But it's so joyful for me to be able to include them in that as well.

What do you think prevents others from achieving a similar balance between travel and work? Do you think it's possible and sustainable?

It's possible, but it depends on individual circumstances and preferences. For some, it involves balancing different income streams or choosing between paid assignments and personal travel. Sometimes, it means setting aside time specifically for work and then enjoying the destination without distractions.

For me, right now that balance looks like trips away where I get to bring my family with me, but it hasn't always been like that. For most of my travel writing career, work travel and family travel have been separated.

We went to Europe recently where we stayed in a hotel and that was hosted [accommodation covered by the venue]. Then I wrote a couple of stories about the city. Then I had a break of two weeks in the middle of that in the United Kingdom where I did no writing, no work. Then at the end, we stayed in Raffles London, again hosted, and I wrote a review for a publication.

This worked for us—a mix of work and then some time fully off. Understanding what works best for your lifestyle is key to achieving this balance.

What advice would you give to someone looking to include more Bleisure in their life, especially through travel writing?

Building and maintaining professional relationships is crucial in the freelance world. Networking and developing strong relationships with editors and publications has added to my success. Be open to opportunities, even those that might initially seem daunting. The willingness to take on challenges has been a significant factor in my writing career success.

What's your dream destination to work in?

While I love traveling, there's something wonderful about returning home. It's my base, and I feel most comfortable and productive there. I've worked in all sorts of places all around the world, including in airplanes. And for me, getting the bulk of my work done at home is how I like to roll. I find it very difficult to do proper work when I'm on the road.

So, it might be controversial, but home is my dream destination to work in.

CONNECT WITH LINDY

- Website: thefreelancersyear.com
- Instagram: @thefreelancersyear
- Hear the full interview with Lindy on my podcast, *The Emma Lovell Show*.

3

SHE HAS THE TRAVEL BUG

As I walked across the white beach sand into the glistening water, I took a moment to look around me and realize where I was on a Thursday morning. A tropical island in North Queensland. As I stood in the water, a frangipani in my hair, the sun beaming down on my face, I threw my head back and laughed.

"This is my life," I said to no one but myself. "I'm traveling and running my business. This is the life I get to live; the life I've created." It was 2012, a few years into my business. But already I had the right idea and had set my course. I knew then it was possible, but I couldn't have imagined how good it could truly get.

TRAVEL IS IN MY BONES

Whenever I'm asked where my next trip is or where I've just been, the comment that quickly follows is, "You've got the travel bug." Like travel is something contagious. Travel isn't something that was sprung on me, like a disease. Travel is a part of my life and has been since day dot. I can't imagine my life without traveling. It fuels me, motivates me and inspires me.

I do not live to work; I work to live. And travel is my guiding light. It's my passion. It's what I love. It's what gets me up in the morning. My love of travel runs deep, and it is difficult to explain how I've embraced the Bleisure life without sharing where it all started.

Let's go back to the beginning.

In 1989, at 22 months old, I took my first international trip. My parents, who emigrated from the U.K., took me and my elder brother, James, back to attend my uncle's wedding. It was my brother's second trip to the U.K. at just 4 years old. We did many trips like this as a family.

Travel is part of my life because it is part of my family's life. To see my extended family in England, I must travel. And they travel to Australia, too. Now, as an adult with a family of my own, I live in Queensland. My younger sister, Andrea, lives here too, but my mum, dad and brother all live in New South Wales—an hour apart from one another. So, to see my family in Australia, I also must travel. But it's not that I must. I choose to travel. I love to travel. I love to visit my family and spend time with them. Relationships and connections fuel my love for travel.

A MIGRANT FAMILY

My parents emigrated to Australia in 1981, thanks to Dad's boss Jim Featherston giving him a chance at a different role. Jim ran a logistics company called Meadows Freight. Mum and Dad were newly married, just 22 and 24 years old. Although daunted, the challenge excited them and they came out for a year as an adventure. And here we are, 43 years later. I came along in 1987. Australia is our home.

MY SECOND HOME

England is a second home to me. I was proud as a kid to say that I am Australian with British blood. I've had people try to tell me I'm British because my parents are, but I think your culture is where you grow up and where your heart is. I love my British heritage and that side of my family, but I am very much Australian in my approach to the world. I like to claim global citizenship, but my anchor will always be Australia.

Do you believe that your body remembers where you have traveled even if your mind does not? On that trip back to the U.K., we visited Japan. For many years I claimed it as a destination despite not remembering it. And when I returned many years later, I felt that physical connection to it.

I have a photo of me playing on the grass in England from that first international trip too. It could be grass anywhere in the world. But I know it's a photo of me in England. I now have a photo of my son from 2022, aged 18 months, sitting on the grass in England. For me that connection is deeply special. Even at his young age, his little body is soaking in the three visits he has made to the U.K so far. He will connect to a country that holds so much heritage and many memories for his family. I love that. I share more about how you can travel with kids in Chapter 13 of this book.

TRAVELING AS A CHILD

As a child, I traveled a lot. Perhaps not a lot by today's standards, but back in the '90s, it was a lot. I recognize what a tremendous investment my parents made in us exploring the world. We did have some little family holidays at camper parks and a Gold Coast holiday when I was six years old—surely a rite-of-passage in most middle-class Aussie kids' lives. But it was our international adventures that stand out in my memory.

- **1996–7:** aged nine, U.S.A. and U.K. for six weeks over the Christmas holidays.
- **1998:** aged 10, Hong Kong to visit my aunty, uncle and cousins, while they were expats.
- **1999:** aged 11, Bali, Indonesia for the best family holiday of our lives. Hands down.

- **2004:** aged 17, U.K. for four weeks, celebrating my parents' silver anniversary.
- **2005:** aged 17, India for a conference with my father, a trip that changed the trajectory of my travels and my working life. More on that later.
- **2003:** aged 16, New Zealand for a 16-day water polo tour, playing teams and being billeted in homes. I was blessed to travel solo at such a young age.
- **2005:** aged 18, "schoolies" cruise. In Australia, students leaving school celebrate "schoolies week." I went without my family but with 2500 other recent school leavers to the Pacific islands of New Caledonia, Lifou Island, Isle of Pines and Mystery Island.

MY SOLO TRAVELS BEGIN

It was time for the real adventures to begin. As you know, I decided at age nine to travel for a year when I finished school. A friend and I vowed we would do the adventure together. But as young friendships go, she soon lost sight of that goal. But I didn't. I held on to that dream in my heart and kept the goal in my mind consistently over the next nine years.

In February 2006, I flew out for my gap year. I visited 13 countries that year. Money was tight, but I worked as much as I could and found extra when I needed it. Like the time I wanted to go to Denmark for a long weekend but couldn't afford it on my office job wage. So, I got a job at a bar for two nights a week, 15 minutes from home. I did that after work for six weeks and paid for my weekend. I made things happen, even at the tender age of 19 years old.

I'm grateful to my family and friends in England, Europe and Asia for helping me to travel on so little money. I lived with my uncle for six weeks, then my grandmother for three months, paying board and having lots of my living costs subsidized. I stayed with friends and their kindness and generosity stays with me. I try to pay this back karmically by helping people less fortunate than me, or as clueless about how far one's travel dollars could go as young Emma was.

I returned to Australia to do my degree, but I had not satisfied my travel appetite. I was just getting started. The long university semester breaks allowed me to travel. In 2007, I planned to work during my Christmas and new year's vacation in the ski fields of Canada. I was off to do a three-month season.

But, by the time the season came along, I hadn't yet saved enough to last me the distance, so I worked a little longer in Australia, and cut the experience back to seven weeks. That's OK. I made a bit of a sacrifice and adapted. I would not give up on the idea because I couldn't do the whole planned time. It was as full, adventurous and exciting as if I'd done the whole season.

OVERSEAS STUDY

My next big travel adventure came in 2009 when I accepted a scholarship to study abroad at El Tec de Monterrey in Monterrey, Mexico. Six months of living, studying and partying at Mexico's premier university. While there, I embraced the joy of the mini trip. We took long weekends—leaving Friday afternoon and coming back before our classes Monday—to explore the cities near and far in Mexico. Once, we took a 15-hour overnight bus to party with 30 close friends in a city called Mazatlán on the coast.

Was it worth it? Absolutely. I loved Mexico and I still say, *Mexico es en mi corazon*, which is probably not how they would phrase it, but I'm saying, "Mexico is in my heart."

As you know, I love to work. And although I didn't necessarily need the money as I was on scholarship and had savings and a personal loan, I couldn't help but find work. Our favorite local students' bar, Cabana, offered me promotions work. The manager quickly identified that we girls knew how to draw a crowd. We earned a commission for all the people who came with us and got free drinks for our role. I didn't make millions, but it certainly subsidized our partying and contributed to some of my gallivanting.

Traveling from Mexico City to the desert of Quattro Cienega, from the jungles of Xilitla to the colonial town of Zacatecas—where we partied in a mine—we packed in what we could. For *semana santa*, meaning spring break, three of us set off on an 18-day adventure from Cancun to Oaxaca and back up to Mexico city. Catching buses and using hire cars to stay in incredible places, we explored the southern border, close to neighboring Guatemala. We visited temples, partied in sandy-floored nightclubs, visited ancient ruins, dove in cenotes (sink-holes), and rode horses through canyons. To say this was a highlight of my life is an understatement. I felt so free and embraced all I came across. Mexico is such a magical place, and I felt connected to both the land and who I was.

SWINE FLU CHANGES MY PLANS

Unfortunately, in April 2009, swine flu arrived in Mexico. I experienced the apocalyptic-like quiet of the streets, the enforcement of masks and the fear of a deadly virus. Later, when COVID-19 struck, it felt all too familiar. Some students didn't take it seriously and loved the extra partying when classes were canceled. Others were fearful and sad, quickly booking flights home to their respective countries.

I felt torn. I wanted to stay in the Mexico I loved. I had a love, *mi novio* (boyfriend). But with all the restrictions, it was no longer the place I loved. I made the tough decision to end my time in Mexico one month early and head over the border to the United States with some friends.

Heartbroken at the change of plans, I felt lost. I worried that perhaps my university back home would not accept the assignments and tests I'd done in Mexico. I went to Plan B: hang out with my brother, who was traveling in the U.S.A for two months and get to know my cousin who he was staying with.

My cousin was my grandmother's cousin, Bill Hunter. He was then 86 years old. Although I still pine for the lost time in Mexico, I am grateful for that month of adventure with my brother and the bond we formed with my cousin Bill and his dear friends. He took us in and showed us such love and kindness. We did much more than our travel budgets would ever have afforded and had money-can't-buy experiences. We attended the qualifying weekend of the Indy 500 with a magician who had performed there for more than 40 years. That magician was my cousin, Bill. Yes, 86 and he was still performing magic for drivers, sponsors and their guests.

JUST SAY YES AND GO WITH IT

Back to Australia in 2009 and … you know what happened. A few months into my return and I landed up on my butt in the snow with a broken back. Time for a long hard look at what the future looked like.

This freedom, this joy, these experiences—I wanted more of them. A broken back and a limiting job would not stop me. A business owner, my own boss, a woman of the world—I had to become that person.

MY TIME, MY WAY

From then on, I made sure I could go anywhere, work from anywhere and do whatever I wanted. Woo-hoo. Now, to keep this record of my travels shorter than a Tolkien novel, I'm going to fast forward and summarize the places I've been. Here are the countries I've visited:

1. Australia
2. Japan
3. U.K.
4. U.S.A.
5. Scotland
6. Hong Kong (at the time part of the U.K., now Republic of China)
7. Indonesia (Bali)
8. New Zealand
9. India
10. New Caledonia
11. Nepal
12. Germany
13. Malaysia
14. Sweden
15. France
16. Spain
17. Austria
18. Denmark
19. The Czech Republic
20. Switzerland
21. Singapore
22. Canada

23. Taiwan (1/2 special territories)
24. South Africa
25. Tanzania
26. Kenya
27. Mexico
28. Thailand
29. Bahamas
30. U.S. Virgin Islands (St. Thomas)
31. Sint Maarten (Dutch colony)
32. Saint Martin (French colony)
33. Bangladesh
34. Peru
35. Bolivia
36. Sri Lanka
37. Borneo
38. Finland
39. Netherlands
40. China
41. Cambodia
42. Vietnam
43. Serbia
44. Uganda
45. Bhutan
46. Fiji
47. U.A.E.
48. Bahrain
49. Hungary
50. South Korea
51. Cuba
52. Iceland
53. Ireland
54. Italy
55. The Vatican (2/2 special territories)
56. Mongolia
57. Papua New Guinea
58. Poland
59. Lithuania
60. Latvia
61. Estonia
62. Brunei
63. Vanuatu
64. Belize
65. Malta
66. Montenegro
67. Bosnia
68. Croatia
69. Albania
70. Belgium
71. Luxembourg
72. Wales

MY NEW TRAVEL MISSION

In 2019, I set myself a new mission: visit every country recognized by the United Nations in the world. There are 193 and two special territories, making 195. Fun fact. I've been to both those special territories: Taiwan and The Vatican.

With 72 countries visited, of which 64 are U.N. recognized, I'm well on the way to achieving that mission. Have these trips all been just for vacations? No, not at all. Some were for work, some were for leisure, some were for adventure and some were for a hybrid of them all.

For the rest of this book, I will share every secret I can about the Bleisure life. The ups and downs, the travel and work hacks, the difficulties and the triumphs.

I want to show you what's possible and how it can work, so that you too can travel the world, make more money and live a life you love now.

Let me get you in the mood.

Questions for reflection

Take out your journal and start creating your travel wish list.

1. What's the destination you'd like to visit the most?

2. Do you keep a list of countries you've visited? If so, how many?

3. What other countries would you like to add to the list in the next five years?

4. What type of travel do you currently enjoy?

5. How often are you taking holidays?

6. How often do you take mini breaks?

7. What's stopping you from traveling more?

8. What would happen if you traveled more?

Great—we're adding more to your Bleisure Life Action Plan with this travel audit and dreaming.

Short and sweet

You know the drill; you don't have time right now but you want to get the gist of this chapter. Here you go:

- I don't have the travel bug. Travel is part of my life.

- My family is from the U.K., so I travel to stay connected with them.

- Gap years are amazing, but they're not the only way to travel.

- Ski seasons are awesome, but they're not the only way to travel.

- Exchange is an incredible way for students to experience travel.

- Travel is something I do for enjoyment but I've made an income from it.

- Yep, I've been to a lot of countries.

- You can experience different types of travel.

- Travel can be for work and leisure—or better, for both. Bleisure.

4

SELF-CARE:
SLOW DOWN TO SPEED UP

WARNING SIGNS

Trigger warning, dear reader. What you read next might be confronting for you.

I'm going to crash my car. This thought wasn't, *Whoops, I'm losing concentration, I might crash if I do.* It was, *If I don't pull over right now, I'm going to crash the car into a wall on purpose.*

I was so broken, so exhausted, so over my work that, for a split second, this seemed like the only solution. It was 2010, just one year from when I had broken my back and I'd now broken my mind. I could see it and feel it but I couldn't stop it.

I managed to stop the car safely in the side road before having a panic attack. My first ever and, hopefully, the worst I will ever have. My heart raced. My breath came in gasps. I felt my mind might break right there in my car. That's something I've focused on never repeating. Not allowing myself to get to that point again.

Are you reading this and thinking, *Yep, I've had those thoughts too*? I mean thoughts about having a minor injury to earn a small hospital stay. Nothing that will permanently damage you. Because I still have thoughts like these from time to time.

I used to think how nice it had been to lie down for eight days when I broke my back. And to rest in the following 10 weeks in a back brace. And even the eight months of physical therapy to recover seemed attractive.

Or when my doctors forced me to rest after my elective cesarean. They told me not to lift anything heavier than my darling baby boy, Finn, and do very little for 12 weeks. Bliss.

However, I had blocked out how painful those events were and how they taxed my body. At those times, I was so mentally broken that being physically broken almost seemed better. Now I recognize these thoughts are a sign that burnout is imminent. I enact a self-care plan immediately. Having self-care as a daily activity—not weekly or monthly—protects my health and happiness in my business and my life.

So please read these words and take note: I would take a broken body over a broken mind any day. You do not have to break physically, mentally or emotionally to …

TAKE A BREAK

The Bleisure life demands a particular attention to self-care. If you, like me, want to mix your personal life with business and travel, you will have to pay more attention than most to looking after your mental, emotional and physical health. When you ditch the boundaries and rules of the broader society, you must set your own boundaries. It's a lesson I learned the hard way. You can take it from me.

WHAT SELF-CARE LOOKS LIKE

But what does self-care mean? Self-care means looking after your mental, physical and emotional health without others having to do it for you. That doesn't mean you don't need support. We all do. It means choosing you, saying "yes" to you.

Everybody's version of self-care looks different. And that is fine. People often think of self-care as getting your nails done, getting a massage or going on a retreat. I advocate for those forms of self-care and I run retreats (more about that later). But self-care doesn't have to be dramatic or involve hours, days or weeks. It can be something simple.

My wonderful client, leadership coach Liz Ellis, practices self-care. Every night Liz makes herself a cup of chai or cacao before bed. Beautiful. It's a simple, consistent ritual she has for herself. She makes it on the stove with a saucepan using organic products. The whole process is part of the routine. She is calm as she goes about each step. She then sits down and enjoys that cup of chai or cacao, indulging in the flavors and taking a moment of quiet before she goes to bed.

I've stayed in Liz's home and she's invited me to take part. It's such a beautiful, loving and simple way to make time and space for yourself. That's what self-care is. Every day, make time and space for yourself and whatever you need.

ANNUAL HOLIDAYS ARE NOT ENOUGH

Of course, you can take holidays. Holidays are great. I'm sure you have done this: you've worked nonstop, then you've gone on holiday. But slaving away for 48 weeks a year, hanging out until you can get away, is unsustainable. You take days to wind down. By the time you start to enjoy your holiday and relax, you have to come back home. And within two days that lovely holiday feeling is gone. So, you do it all again. You work, work, work, and save up to take a holiday. Work again. Holiday. Exhausting. That is not the Bleisure life.

Burnout gets more attention in the business world now than ever before. It's been around for a long time. But we have given it a name and recognize the signs of it. Well, hypothetically we recognize it. Unfortunately, we often only see the signs once we're already in it. Even then, it often takes a friend, client or colleague—someone like my dear Liz—to tell you, "Hey, I think you're approaching or are already in burnout."

I sometimes hear other people telling me:

"Just take care of yourself."
"Just be kind to yourself."
"Just do this…"
"Just do that…"

Of course, such advice is not *helpful* when you're overwhelmed. But if you can learn to use it as a reminder for yourself, you can trigger a self-care regime.

MORE HOLIDAYS, MORE OFTEN

If you take care of yourself, you can avoid burnout. Take a bit of a holiday all the time. That is the Bleisure life. You are going to get good at this. But the simple choices seem the hardest, right?

I remember telling a colleague that getting to bed on time is challenging for me. But ask me to go to India, and I'll jump on a plane with ease.

For me, self-care is living on the Gold Coast. Here I feel like I am on holiday all the time. I get in the water, sit in the sun or go for a walk. That's my version of self-care.

Your Bleisure doesn't have to be that big. When you live a Bleisure life, you find the activities you love and do them every day. When you read a book, you sit down and absorb it. You choose basic activities to top up your tank and support you.

SELF-CARE IN A CRISIS

Create space

There will always be times when life is busy. It frustrates me when I'm in one of those seasons and there's a lot on. I accept it's a short season and I must get on with it. You might have an event or a launch to attend or be at the final stages of a project. Or life throws a spanner in the works.

In 2023, two dear girlfriends passed away from breast cancer within three weeks. They had both lived with breast cancer for a few years, but I had expected they would recover. Unfortunately, they both became worse. The loss and the intense grief hit me and I wasn't prepared. I felt devastated.

When the news came, I was touring several Australian cities, moving every few days over eight weeks, taking part in and hosting events, hosting photoshoots, and launching my new business brand. I lost my two friends in the middle of the tour. What to do? I could cancel the tour, sure. But I knew I would feel worse if I canceled and had nothing to do.

Or I could create more space.

Whenever I could, I asked people for space and grace. I shared my feeling as best as I could, asked for help and moved events around to give me breathing space. For example, I shifted a conference gig to noon instead of nine in the morning. I missed some speakers and sessions. I love networking and meeting people at events. But that day I needed to stay longer in bed. To cry, to rest, to wallow, to nurture my heart and my soul. Once I gave myself that time and space, I knew that being around people and staying committed to the event for the afternoon would feel better. I was right.

People tried to help me with advice about what I "could" do. I replied, "Don't you worry. I'm doing all those things." But the biggest self-care act in a crisis is just to be, not do. What's the best way to just be and not do when I feel overwhelmed? I go to sleep.

Go to sleep

In the Bleisure life, we prioritize sleep. In bed. On the plane. In a crisis. (I sit here at 11:16 p.m. reading these words mocking me as I type. Don't worry, I'll go to bed soon. I have a sleep-in planned tomorrow. Woo-hoo, thank you, in-laws.)

When I feel the familiar signs of burnout and need to sleep, I do whatever I must. I leave my phone in another room. I take some melatonin or magnesium or both. I drink herbal tea, take a late-night bath or a hot shower, use my Lush sleep spray, and put on my Lush sleep body cream. I get into bed early and rest even without sleep to help me through the next day, week or season.

A bedtime routine and self-care activities make me feel better each day. I top up the tank a bit more and build on that foundation. I'm not always great at it. There's nothing more annoying than someone saying, "Go to bed." I feel like a toddler. But sometimes, it's what I need.

Put boundaries around your time

Self-care is choosing to care for yourself first. So, instead of allowing people to book into my calendar across the workweek, I set boundaries. At the start of the week, I said, "No. I have to focus on my business and catch up." I made time to socialize, travel and do in-person work with my clients at the end of the week. I set boundaries to get this book written and delivered into your hot little hands. That's self-care.

> **BOUNDARIES MEAN SAYING A SMALL NO FOR A GREATER YES**
>
> Say "yes" to you first, put your activities in the calendar first, and then build everybody else's needs and activities around yours.

Eat nourishing food (at least occasionally)

When you're traveling in and out of airports, choosing healthy food can go out the window. Honestly speaking, eating healthy and nourishing food isn't my strong point. I don't find nutrition and food easy. But I know that when I eat well, I feel better for it. Or at least I don't feel like crap.

This works best when I make small adjustments and try to choose better food options. Ask myself, "What does my body need?" If you want to live a sustainable Bleisure life, ask yourself, "Does my body need a little less coffee? Can I cut back on alcohol? Does my body need more vegetables?" Rather than restricting or limiting your diet, choose healthy, nourishing food.

MARTYRDOM IS SO LAST CENTURY

Self-care was foreign to my mother's generation. I have no blame or judgment. Our society simply didn't recognize the impact that lack of self-care and rest had. It wasn't "the done thing" as mum used to say. You got on and took exhaustion on the chin. You pushed through the burnout because hey, everyone was in the same boat. That hasn't changed all that much, but today we burn out at work rather than on home duties. Or both.

I want to learn from that. I don't want to be a martyr. I don't want to resent my husband, my son, my clients and all those around me because I'm not looking after myself. I get massages, a blow-dry or my nails done. And I build in small "holidays." The walk. The swim. The little acts of self-care as I go.

I've been told by some people, specifically my friend Kelley, that self-care is something I do well. Kelley's a mother of two teens and self-care was not a familiar concept. She has rarely traveled alone for pleasure and didn't invest in things that were just for her. Kelley told me that seeing me take some time away from my son at such a young age and choosing myself, inspired and encouraged her to do more for herself. It's a joy to see her rediscovering what she enjoys doing now and making time for herself.

Maybe you're thinking "Oh, well that's nice for you Emma. You have the time and money to look after yourself." I make the time. That is the point. And I decide that self-care is worth spending money on. I also choose to have time away from my son, who I love dearly, while he has cherished time with other loved ones. If you want the Bleisure life, you can make these choices too.

I set aside $100 or $150 a month for self-care rituals that make me feel good. And by committing the money, I make the time. To make that choice, I sacrifice some spending on:

- Clothes.
- Alcohol.
- Nights out.
- Ubers.
- Something I saw on Facebook, Instagram and so on.

WHEN YOU TAKE CARE OF YOU, YOU TAKE CARE OF OTHERS

When I am accountable to myself, I am better for those around me. I go to the gym because I have a virtual personal trainer, Nikki Ellis from Cinch Training, keeping me accountable. Nikki created a 20-minute workout for me. She knows I struggle to dedicate an hour. I can fit 20 minutes into my day.

For my husband, Mathew, going to the gym is self-care. He feels better once he's there. If he doesn't go, he berates himself about lack of time or tiredness or his busy schedule. I suggest he make the time. It's his choice.

BLEISURE PARENTS

When Mathew takes care of himself, we're in a better place together. We both do things for ourselves that we enjoy and fill our cups. When I make time for myself, I show him he can do it too. It's something I do for myself, and advocate for both of us. It shows we can both have our own time and get our needs met especially now that we are parents.

It's also important for me to have quality time away from my son, Finn, so I can be myself, Emma, the human adult person. I have people to help so I can get that self-care now. His grandparents spend time with Finn. We don't call it babysitting; it's precious quality time and a privilege to share in his life. I ask friends if he can have a playdate so I can do something for myself. I have friends with teenage children who have never gone away for a night or for a weekend, without the kids. I feel grateful for the help I have. But I make choices and have hard conversations and set boundaries. And I stand up for myself and ask for what I need. That is a true act of self-love and self-care.

I say to my husband, "I need you to take Finn out in the morning so that I can have an extra hour of sleep because I'm just not coping." Self-care is saying, "I need someone to help me with shopping so I can cook some nourishing food. Let's eat more vegetables." That's me asking for help and asking for what I need to take care of myself.

There are seasons of life where we are in greater demand. Finn is a toddler. He needs me. My family has been in crisis while my nephew was terminally ill. There's just more giving and energy needed. But this is a time when self-care is more important than ever.

Even when there's so much going on, I stay committed to the Bleisure life, and I build in time to sleep, to eat well, to do what I love. This year, I feel called to spend more time around horses. When I was asking myself what I needed, what came to mind was, "I want to be around horses." My goal is to go horse riding more often. It's something I've always enjoyed, and my inner child wants that joy.

Horses mean freedom, beauty, strength. They are graceful, wild and free. They're calming but also fun. And little girl Emma always wanted a horse. Being around them now satisfies her. It's something I love and enjoy, so I'm going to do it. It's a new and fun way for me to experience self-care.

SHOW OTHERS YOU LOVE YOURSELF

It's a win that people have recognized I do self-care well. Don't get me wrong, I still have times when it's hard, times where everything gets in the way. Work and other people take over. My boundaries go out the window and my needs, wants and desires fall by the wayside. Then I remember my boundaries and the psychologist's message I wrote on the wall years ago: "Say 'no' to their needs so you can say 'yes' to yours."

'Say 'no' to their needs so you can say 'yes' to yours.'

My affirmation card says: "Your boundaries are as much for other people's safety as they are for yours. Defend them without hesitation or guilt."

Of course, travel is the ultimate self-care for me. I get inspiration, ideas and joy from my travels. That's why travel is a huge part of my life. I prioritize travel throughout the weeks and months of the year. Whether it's with my husband and son, for business events, in groups or solo, I love all the different varieties of travel. Each type tops up my self-care tank.

For the Bleisure artist, self-care is getting the time to be free, to explore, to be inspired, to be motivated to dream, and to wander and have new experiences.

YOUR DAILY BLEISURE SELF-CARE CHECKLIST

As I wrap up this chapter, I'm going to ask you just one question. In the interests of self-care, we will keep it simple.

I encourage you to determine your self-care priorities from this checklist. It's a list of ways to take care of yourself and, therefore, those you love. Choose three activities from this list—or add your own—that you will do just for you, no matter where in the world you are. Write them down. Can't afford the gym or don't like it? Don't do it. If you don't like yoga, don't do it. If you hate baths, don't take them. If you're not into getting your nails done, then don't. Choose what is right for you.

- Go for a walk. That's one of my favorite easy self-care wins.
- Call a friend. Reach out and discuss where you're at.
- Have a bath.
- Book a massage.
- Drink a cup of warm milk before bed.
- Go on a retreat (your own or someone else's).
- Read a book or the newspaper.
- Spend a day at the spa.

- Go to an unfamiliar environment—from a beach to a shopping center.
- Learn something new.
- Go out for a night with the girls or the guys.
- Take your loved one on a date.
- Play games. For my husband, Mathew, self-care is playing video games. He also plays the tabletop mini war game, Warhammer, with his friends. I love that he has something that's just for him and I tell him so. I'm also a bit mean and call him a "nerd." And he admits it is nerdy and calls his Warhammer pieces his "war dollies."

YOUR CRISIS SELF-CARE PLAN

How will you look after yourself in a crisis? Look at the strategies I used and think this through. Do you want to stop everything or create space? What will you say to others and how will you say it? It's easier to practice before the fact.

Short and sweet

Too busy to remember it all? Here's your summary:

- Self-care is not selfish; it's essential for living a life you love.

- Slow down big time to live the Bleisure life or face burnout.

- You don't have to break yourself physically, emotionally or mentally—a forced break—to take a break. Build breaks into everyday life.

- Self-care isn't just pampering yourself, although that is good. It's about daily habits that keep you healthy. Like a nightly ritual of making chai or cacao to chill out.

- Consistently practice self-care.

- Be ready to add extra self-care in a crisis.

- Recognize burnout signs early and start a plan to take care of yourself, step by step, day by day.

- Self-care looks different for everyone and that's OK. Complete the checklist to find out what it looks like for you.

VALERIE KHOO
Multi-passionate
entrepreneur

We all have a hero we look up to or want to meet one day. Author, artist and entrepreneur Valerie Khoo is that person for me. In her book, *Power Stories: The 8 Stories You Must Tell to Build an Epic Business*, Valerie shares that rock star Jon Bon Jovi is that person for her. And she got to interview him during her magazine career.

I met Valerie in 2012 at the Melbourne Writers Group. "You are my Bon Jovi," I said to her.

Valerie is the chief executive officer of the Australian Writers' Centre. She is also an artist who paints large-scale floral artworks. She hosts the top-rating podcast *So You Want to Be a Writer*.

I admire and respect business leaders. Valerie is an incredible writer, entrepreneur and mentor. I'm delighted to now call her a friend and to have incredible conversations about things we both love—business and travel.

To have read your business hero's book and now have them in your book is mind blowing. I'm crying as I type this because 12 years ago I could not have imagined this moment. Thank you, Valerie.

Can you start by describing your job or business?

I am passionate about creativity. I also love the idea that people have the potential to follow their dreams and don't have to be pigeonholed into one area. I love writing, art, music, cats and a whole lot more. I'm a CEO but also have a parallel career as an artist. I'm obsessed with the idea that we all need to follow our creative curiosity to find fulfillment in life. I mentor creatives and corporate escapees to find a life that's full of purpose where they can earn a healthy income and feed their creative soul.

As CEO and founder of the Australian Writers' Centre, which is the leading center in providing writing courses, I help people and mentor those who want to get published, write with confidence or change careers, especially those who come to us later in life. Besides that, I am also a visual artist with an art and design business, creating original paintings and designs for wallpaper, upholstery fabrics and so on. Additionally, I am a board director of a small bank, where I get heavily involved in the world of banking and finance. So, these are the three main buckets of my professional life.

Do you think of yourself as an entrepreneur?

Oh, yeah, for sure. I guess that's the overriding term that would be appropriate. And then there are all the little things that come in— well, not little; some of them are big things. I'm also open to other opportunities that I'm passionate about, but at the moment, my plate is pretty full.

You often speak about the importance of diversifying your income. Can you elaborate on that?

It's important but it's not just about having multiple ways of making income. It's about diversifying your risk. It's about spreading your risk across a wide range of income sources. So, if one thing is going slow, you can focus on another thing that is picking up or going well. It's a good way to ensure consistency overall, even if it's not consistent within each individual stream.

How did you get started with your current way of working?

When I started freelancing, it was mainly freelance writing. I was in jobs before that, working in glossy magazines and companies. Even when I was working for them, I had ideas I wanted to pursue outside of work, not necessarily for money but out of interest. When I left full-time employment, I took baby steps, starting with a three-day-a-week gig and freelancing the rest of the time to ease into it.

❝When you love what you do, you naturally get better at it and people will pay you for it.❞

Freelancing allowed me to diversify into different types of writing and explore various interests, which led to multiple streams of income.

There's no greater time [than now for entrepreneurs] to try different things because it's so much easier to set a website up, create a social media profile and reach heaps of people.

Do you love travel, and how do you include it in your work?

I love new experiences and learning, which is intensified when you travel. It's not the act of getting on a plane or carrying bags that I love, but the experiences at the other end. I enjoy learning about history, culture, food and languages. Pre-pandemic, I traveled a lot for work, going to cities for [writing and speaking] gigs and leaving immediately after. I had a system for each city where I would do something I enjoyed, like booking a theater show in Brisbane. Post-pandemic, I travel differently. I want to travel for learning and experiences rather than just for work commitments.

What advice would you give for someone to include more travel in their work or life?

It's about thinking outside the box and combining personal interests with professional opportunities.

How do you make time for self-care and find balance in your schedule?

Sometimes I forget about self-care because I enjoy what I'm doing and like getting things done. But it's important to be aware and consciously incorporate rest into your routine. I don't have all the answers and I'm still working on it. For me, switching off and downtime look different depending on the situation.

Do you think the Bleisure life—combining business and leisure—is sustainable?

Absolutely. It's important to do what you love. When you love what you do, you naturally get better at it and people will pay you for it.

Doing what you love is vital for your soul and helps you excel, which in turn brings in a good income.

I'm combining [my trip to the Riviera] with a series of art workshops and art classes … because it's a great combination of business and pleasure.

What's your dream destination to work in?

I actually love working at home. But my dream is to have a comfortable mobile office that allows me to work by beautiful water bodies and then return home to my bed. The idea is to have all my work essentials in a van, so I can enjoy incredible views while working and still have the comforts of home.

CONNECT WITH VALERIE

- Website: valeriekhoo.com
- Instagram: @valeriekhoo
- Hear the full interview with Valerie on my podcast, *The Emma Lovell Show.*

5

DIVERSIFY YOUR INCOME STREAMS

Job interviewer: *"What's the biggest challenge you've ever faced?"*

Me: *"I cycled through Vietnam for eight days, covering over 300 kilometers, with 32 Dutch women, riding nonstop for 10 hours per day."*

Job interviewer: *"You're hired."*

Or that's how I imagine it would go if I ever had to go for a job interview. I've maybe been to five in my life and some of those were in my teens. But yes, if any employer for any job wants to see if I'm up to a challenge, this example—and my work history—proves I have got grit.

I'm not afraid of hard work or challenging problems. Or working to earn an experience like I did when I managed that cycling tour. And I like making money. This book isn't about not working. It's about making money in the smartest and the most time and energy efficient ways possible. Ways that light you up but also ways that give you an experience you want without having to pay for it. It's about getting an income through experiences or in a "value exchange," by which I mean exchanging skills for payment in a currency other than money.

But let's go back a step. Why on earth was I managing a tour of 32 Dutch women cycling through Vietnam? Well, I was working with a charity challenge company at the time and they gave me the opportunity of managing the cycle tour in 2014. I was 26 years old. I accepted because I would get an amazing, bucket list experience in exchange for my adventure, leadership and organizational skills. And they paid all my expenses. My only expenses back home were my rent and basics, but you pay for that when you go on holiday anyway. They covered my food and accommodation. I spent very little on the tour. And I even got a tip on that Vietnam trip, which covered my massage and nails pamper treat at the end. So, I got paid, even if it was a small amount.

But work I did.

I found that these Dutch women were not ones to mince their words. And due to some poor communication about my role and the package, the women were unclear that I was the leader of the group. But, once they realized, they made me the first point of contact for any grievances they had. And after Day One there were many. These included:

- The roads were too modern and paved.
- We weren't riding in the rice paddies as the photos showed. (Yep, they're wet; it doesn't work like that.)
- The hotels were too nice.
- We weren't cycling enough.
- We had to go in a vehicle to get to the first cycle point; we were meant to be cycling the whole time.
- It rained.
- The overnight train was late.
- The food wasn't adventurous enough because we ate in the hotels we stayed in.
- It wasn't "real" Vietnam.

I sat and listened to the list of complaints. Then I reinforced the message I had explained from the beginning: "expect the unexpected."

I sent a four-page report back to the tour-organizing headquarters to bring them up to date.

It got worse before it got better. Fast forward a few days, and I struggled to get along with our local head guide, who had a poor grasp of English and refused to communicate with me. He was replaced by the head of the local tour company, who joined our trip to assist me. Injuries happened left, right and center. At one point, the road hadn't been checked before the tour, and the cycle down the hill was treacherous. Half the women ended up in the support vehicle. Then the women stopped listening to our guides, overtaking them. I ended one leg of the tour pulling everyone over on the side of the road to explain safety 101 and threatening to cancel the cycling altogether. Both I and the participants ended up in tears.

And then the tour was over and the 32 Dutch women, me and my assistant ended up jumping up and down in a karaoke bar, singing along to Britney Spears and Aerosmith. I couldn't love these women harder if I tried.

And that's what work can look like for me. I may not have had the money to spend on a trip like that on my business income at the time. But I was willing to diversify my income and to see the exchange as another way of paying my way.

Challenging? *Yes.*

Memorable? *Yes.*

Would I do it again? *Yes and I have.*

Is it work? *Absolutely, yes.*

Is the compensation worth it? *At that time of my life, yes.*

Now with a husband and child and as the travel for my business and personal activities increases, I am more discerning about the adventures I take on. But at 26, traveling the world for free, building valuable leadership skills, gaining lifelong friends—including the then 75-year-old Betsy, my darling and one of the fiercest and most fabulous women I've ever met—and memories that last a lifetime? Yes, it was worth it.

ADOPT THE INCOME DIVERSITY ATTITUDE

So, you might be sitting there going, "Oh, but I have my job and that's it for how I can make money. I'm limited to traveling only as a holiday."

Nope. Not true. This was a way that I "worked" for my trip. Yes, in recent years, I've preferred to earn my money and choose how and when I travel. Unless a colleague comes to me and says, "Do you want to manage a trek to Mount Kilimanjaro for a charity you love and support?" Well, then, I'd say "yes" and leap at the chance again.

One key to my longevity in business and travels is diversifying my income streams. I'm not suggesting it's easy to travel the world and money will just come to you. But I am saying you can live the dream, and work is part of creating a life you love. It's how you work that makes the difference.

Recognizing where income flows into my life makes me energized and excited to go after more. I recommend tracking all your money and income. It's an incredible exercise in abundance and gratitude.

POTENTIAL INCOME STREAMS

Let's go through the many ways I've worked. By sharing this, I hope to inspire you to explore other options for your own income and experiences. I've kept the list in somewhat of a chronological order throughout my career, so you can see how I have progressed. But many of these roles were held simultaneously—that's the idea with multiple income streams.

Client work

I make money in my business with client work: coaching, training and speaking. As well, I have copywriting, social media, public relations and marketing skills. If I ever need additional income, I can do gig work in these areas. Copywriting is the easiest for me to pick up.

I started working freelance gigs and registered with the Australian Tax Office as a sole trader. That means I don't employ any staff. It's easy to set up an Australian Business Number (ABN) and to work under your own name. And you can do a lot online from anywhere in the world.

You might have a skill set where you work a full-time role and then do extra client work outside of hours. Think about the skill sets you have. Could you get some client work?

Promotions

Promotions were a big part of my working life and I got into it at 19 years old. My high school friend was a model and cheerleader and had been doing casual promotions work alongside her entertainment gigs. I started by contacting the promotions agency she was working with. I loved the flexibility of this work and ended up working with eight agencies, to increase my opportunities for work and keep my diary full. I also worked directly for clients, not through an agency, such as the fruit juice company Nudie Juice.

As long as you have an ABN, you can pick up this type of work, which can be anything from handing out flyers at bus stops to giving out samples of butter in supermarkets to promoting a car brand, such as Hyundai, outside the Melbourne Cricket Ground (MCG) during an Aussie Rules football match.

This work is available all over Australia, the U.K. and many other countries. I picked up promotions work for a bar in Mexico and earned income and free entry and drinks. Fabulous, as I was a student then.

Promotional work gave me the opportunity to travel. Here's some examples of jobs over the years:

- Representing a large phone company at a huge annual car race in Bathurst, New South Wales.
- Promoting dog food at the annual agricultural show in Canberra, Australia's capital.
- Handing out energy drinks at a big music festival in Melbourne, Victoria.

- Traveling around rural Victoria, helping rural firefighters educate people on bushfire and home safety.

- Entertaining people at three in the morning, lining up outside a telephone store for the launch of a new iPhone.

- Traveling around beaches in a luxury car handing out sim cards for a mobile brand.

- Driving around in a black jeep to ski fields handing out free sample soft drinks, and skiing for free over the weekend.

- Dressing up in a supermarket as broccoli.

- Traveling to bars in Sydney representing a brand of rum and handing out fun prizes.

- Representing a car brand at a car show in Sydney for 10 days— great money, but long days.

In Australia, you will be paid an hourly rate with superannuation on top depending on the role. Weekend shifts attract additional payments, which can add a lot.

This is a fantastic income for a young student or any travelers. You do not have to be a bikini-clad model. This work is available to people of all ages. I never wore a bikini. Black pants, ballet flats and polo shirt. That's the go-to promo look I knew. I'd still do promo work these days if a fun campaign came up. I've worked with so many wonderful people. On a call with a young traveler struggling to find work in Melbourne, I suggested this type of work. "Why not take a break from the work you are qualified for and do some fun work that pays well and allows you to meet a lot of people?"

I also used these skills to run promotional campaigns for client companies. For one family-run milk brand, I asked my friends and sister to dress up in cow suits and they ended up on morning TV. Priceless.

Sub-contracting

Sub-contracting is where you do the work, but it's for your client's client. You get the pay, but you don't have to manage the client. This is a great way to start building a business. It means you can focus on your skill set and not the more challenging part of running any business, which is managing clients. Managing clients includes meeting the client to take a brief, provide a quote, receive feedback on the work and so on.

You get paid a lot less than the business owner who manages the client, but it's also a lot less hassle for you. You do the work, deliver the work and get paid.

And you will learn how to pitch, brief and manage by observing the person who is contracting you. Often, they will mentor you if you're new to the game. You can sub-contract to agencies, writers, PR companies and, as I did, to travel companies.

You'll also need an ABN for this work, and to develop your networking skills. You need lots of contacts with businesses to pick up sub-contracting work. My first role came through the wonderful Johanna Baker-Dowdell and her PR company, Strawberry Communications. I learned so much about the PR world and managing clients. I came full circle when I entered the AusMumpreneur awards in 2023 and won Bronze for Coach of the Year; the awards were the first ever sub-contract gig I worked on through Joh, way back in 2011.

Sub-contracting is wonderful for income, skill development, and building relationships and contacts.

Travel writing

As mentioned, I write copy in my business and as a sub-contractor. But travel writing is different. This is closer to freelance journalism, and it's something I've picked up from time to time. I've been a paid travel writer since 2012 after I did a travel writing course at the Australian

Writers' Centre, founded by Valerie Khoo, who you can read more about in this book (see page 76).

If you can write, and you're willing to learn about publications, to pitch relevant stories and craft an article, then you can earn from travel writing. There are many publications that accept travel articles; sometimes ones you wouldn't even expect, such as a bridal magazine. Yes, they too need travel stories. Some publications I've written for are *The Australian* newspaper, Virgin Australia magazine, Unearth Women, She Defined e-zine, and Travel Bulletin to name a few.

It's not easy to win travel writing gigs as lots of people would love to do it, but it's not impossible. As you are reading my book, you know I have a gift for writing. But writing is also a skill that can be learned. Take a businesslike approach to do well in this industry: that means building relationships with editors and publications, researching before pitching, editing your work so it's ready for print, and delivering your articles by deadline. And as with all business, communication is key.

Note, the longer the story, the more you will be paid. I've also had free or discounted tickets and experiences and received perks for my role as a writer such as 50% off hotels, free products and discounted car rental. Travel writing also makes some of my travel tax deductible.

If this is something you're interested in, you will learn more about the art of travel writing from my interview with travel and food writer Lindy Alexander, on page 46 of this book.

Tutoring, lecturing or running workshops

This can be a great way to use your own experience and skills to help others, while also earning an additional income. Personally, I've not tutored or lectured but have considered both as income streams at various times.

You can host workshops yourself under your own brand, or you may be contracted through a company. You will often need to schedule these outside work hours to meet your audience's needs but also to fit in with your other work, unless it becomes your primary offering. I hosted social media workshops at libraries and a friend's office in the evenings while doing a full-time contract at World Vision Australia and earned a good fee for each attendee per workshop.

My brother is great at mathematics and has been tutoring mathematics students since he was 17. At 38, he still tutors to earn additional income for his family. One of my cousins is also a tutor, putting his excellent piano playing to good use and helping students prepare for their final music exams. If you are gifted in a particular subject or skill, such as a musical instrument or a second language, this can be a great way to earn extra money.

Lecturing can be done through universities, colleges and some other learning institutions such as TAFE here in Australia. A number of my colleagues do this as an additional income for one semester of the year and it's something I'll be open to in my future.

Investments

I am talking about shares, property and more. Investments are a big part of my next five-year plan. I plan to build a foundation of wealth for me and my family by investing in a variety of areas. That is called diversified investment.

Just before publishing this book, I made a good profit from selling my investment property, which I had owned for seven years. The way I bought this house and later sold it has been so interesting to people that I've included an entire case study on how I did it (see page 104).

It took me a long time to realize that my tenant's rent was income. I had a 30-year mortgage and so felt like the money just belonged to the house, but this was a fortnightly income stream (even if the bulk went to the mortgage). Recognizing the rent as income shifted my perspective on investing, and I could see that it was paying dividends already.

I've only just bought my first shares and I'm so excited. I decided to go for something fun and interesting, also high risk because my appetite for risk is high, and so I invested in a new start-up called Got Cakey. We've also put funds into an investment account for my son with a goal to grow this to a tidy nest egg by the time he's 21. That will give him a head start with property investment or whatever he pursues.

I wish I had understood earlier that I could save, spend, have debt and invest all at once, but more on that later. I'm excited to see how this income stream grows as I explore it more.

Casual work

Getting a casual job in a shop, restaurant, cafe, theme park, laboring, warehousing and more is a great way to boost your income.

I worked at a supermarket during COVID-19. Yep, I did casual work as recently as 2020. When COVID-19 hit, I didn't know what would happen. After experiencing the effects of a 2009 swine flu pandemic in Mexico when I lived there, I knew that the impact could last a while.

I didn't want to reach out to people and try to sell them stuff. That felt icky and weird. A friend told me that a supermarket near her in Ballina, New South Wales needed extra staff. The shops were going crazy as people stocked up on supplies.

I drove from the Gold Coast to Ballina—an hour and a half's drive—and stayed at night with my friend's grandmother who lived nearby. I'd work for a few days, then go home again. I did this for two weeks until the borders closed.

The work was pleasant and light on my brain. I think about so much in my business. I'm everything in my business. At the supermarket, I picked up boxes of apples and displayed them. Or took the fruit boxes, packed them down and tidied the shelves. Simple. This was such a reset.

They told me I was doing a great job, so helpful to them. I loved those few weeks. I said, "Please keep me on the books." I would have done a shift once every two weeks or every so often.

Picking up some casual work is a great way to make extra money, either short term or for a consistent top-up of your business income.

I also did this in the U.K. I worked in a bar two nights a week for six weeks to pay for a trip to Denmark for five days. A little extra work for a fab trip and lifelong memories.

Cleaning

My first cleaning role was working as a housekeeper in a hotel in the ski fields of Big White, Canada. It was fun to see that side of tourism, all the foreigners working so we could embrace the snow life. I did it for seven weeks and it was all good. Making beds while looking out at a winter wonderland ain't challenging work. (But I no longer make beds and pay someone else to do it. Ha ha.) I also did this when I first moved to Melbourne, helping a friend's aunty when I had a couple of hundred dollars in my bank account.

If things got tight, I'd do this work again. It's always available; cleaners are in such demand. You could pick up this work in a second. And you can do it anywhere in the world.

Dropping off flyers

Desperate after a shocking tax bill, I went to an online jobs site and found this role: $80 for 1000 flyers. Easy, I thought. I can listen to music, get exercise and get paid. But do you know how many flyers there are? And how far you must walk when you add up all the streets? I ended up calling my then boyfriend Mathew (now my husband) crying, lying (not my finest hour) about a family emergency and dropped back the rest of the flyers. I didn't get paid and I did not care.

I swallowed my pride, asked Mathew for a loan, and went on a payment plan with the Australian Tax Office. My psychologist helped me to manage the shame and get out of crisis mode. Many businesses get big tax bills and aren't prepared for them when they grow. Many take on a tax payment plan. Thankfully, I had good people around me to guide me with this decision.

I do not recommend this work. But sometimes, money is money. You can do it.

But don't.

Speaking and emceeing

Both are a super fun way to work, if I do say so myself. I've been emceeing since I was 17 when I was asked to host the drama competition at school. That is what an emcee (master of ceremonies) does; they host an event, introducing guests, relaxing the crowd and keeping the show moving. I loved it so much and I knew I had a skill—the "gift of the gab"—in my ability to speak confidently in public.

Speaking onstage is a skill you can learn, and confidence is a muscle you can build. My first paid speaking gig came through a promotions agency in about 2012. I couldn't believe I could be paid to speak. Something I do a lot. Every day.

Since then, the gigs have gotten bigger and better. I've spoken for an hourly rate, and I've spoken for gift vouchers. I've also spoken for free or for tickets to an event. I'm booked next year to emcee a huge conference and exhibition event in India, my second gig with them. I first spoke on the stage for this client in 2014, which was a whirlwind and amazing, and only now do I reflect on what a big deal that was.

Although I have spoken for free, I recommend you ask for a fee. Even if it's covering expenses, travel and accommodation. It's a good energetic exchange and will help you feel confident in asking for more each time. Because speakers and emcees add enormous value to events. And you're worth it. So am I.

Mystery shopping

Mystery shopping is a fun one. You get a brief, follow the guidelines, act as a normal customer or shopper, and then you write a report about it. And you get paid for going. And you get free products or services. A magnesium bath, groceries. A Pilates class. And if you have to work, it may as well be fun. And yes, I still do this work now. But shh.

It's a secret. I might have to start wearing wigs and sunglasses to do this when I'm an international bestselling author. Manifesting.

You can register with mystery shopping agencies. There's one here in Australia called Human Experience, run by my friend Nic McClanachan.

Pet sitting

Pet sitting is looking after people's pets. You either stay in someone's home or you have the pet stay with you. You get to have adorable cuddles and get paid for it. It's great.

You can do this in exchange for free accommodation at their home. However, you may also get paid if you sign up to one of the many websites or apps that match sitters with work. Pet sitting reduces your expenses. I had no housing costs at one point, and that is how I bought my house (see "How I bought a house in just seven months on page 104.)

In fact, I set up a pet sitting business, Lovelly Pet Sitters, in one day. I bartered to get my logo done—one client was a graphic designer—so I did three days of puppy care in exchange for my logo design. I was living in Sydney, but I did pet sits in Melbourne, the Gold Coast and Brisbane. As I became more successful, I employed a team to give me more time for my freelance writing and Lovelly Communications work. I built the business to 20 sitters across four cities in three different Australian states, and even one international sitter in Los Angeles.

I stopped running the business in 2019 as my coaching and communication business was growing fast. Also, my husband and I wanted our own pet and got one: a cat named T'Challa.

You don't need to climb to these dizzy heights, but you will need an ABN to sign up to these sites. There are some great apps and websites you can join. This work is available all over the world and can provide a great way to travel.

We are considering doing this again as a family in the next few years so we can travel for longer and experience the local side of some cities. It's a skill I'll always have and a fun way to make some extra cash or stay for free.

And some houses we stayed in were rather luxe: backing onto golf courses, modern apartments in North Sydney, lush pools and more. Why not?

Doing surveys online

This is low paying, so this is for when every dollar counts. You sign up with a survey company and complete the surveys that big brands use to make decisions. You can complete surveys in your PJs in front of the telly in your spare time, so it's easy. Google "jobs completing surveys online" and away you go.

Selling items from your home

I've sold furniture, clothes and a wedding gift online (sorry not telling, ha ha). I've even sold gold jewelry I no longer wore or wanted. There's value in objects that no longer serve you and thanks to places like Facebook marketplace, Etsy and eBay, you can get these items online and find buyers.

My friend, the gorgeous Amanda, was in a financial funk. I suggested she shift the energy and bring in some income any way she could. "Have you got gold?" I asked. Turns out, she had a couple of pieces she never wore and had bad juju for her. They alone were worth several hundred dollars. Just sitting there. She was over the moon and I was too. What a win.

Competitions

People think no one ever wins, but they do. I've won thousands of dollars in prizes, but also in cash. I've been on the radio and won money. I've also won through magazines and online. I once won a trip to the snow worth thousands. Entries that require 25 words or less are my jam. My goal is to one day win a car. Manifesting is something

I believe in, so I get more and more specific about what that car will look like and how it will feel when I win it. That is how to manifest a win. I've also won free concert tickets, meal vouchers, raffle prizes. It's not gambling; it's being in it to win it. And for something you need, it can be so helpful.

My husband is even into it now and I often manifest wins through him. We tag each other on Instagram whenever we see a competition, and a friend has now joined in too. She won a blow dry for two at a hairdresser in our beautiful local shopping center. She invited me to go because I tagged her. Win.

Retreats

I travel to luxurious locations with amazing people and I get paid. Yes, this is what retreats are. There's more to it than that, but I love this way of making money because it is the ultimate in Bleisure. Combining business, travel and self-care. I get as much out of hosting these retreats as my clients get from coming to them. It's such a transformative experience.

You can host retreats too. And I teach you how in Chapter 12 on page 206.

Assisting another professional

You may not have the skills to go out on your own as a business or may not want to. But you may be quite good at something or just helpful. You can be an assistant to a professional, such as a photographer, speaker, event organizer or more.

I assisted the fabulous photographer Jade Warne and incredible speaker Shelly Horton with their group workshops. I earn a commission for each person who attends the day.

You might get paid an hourly rate for attending and assisting with tasks, such as moving furniture around the workplace, getting drinks, helping set up, taking behind-the-scenes footage and more.

Do you know a professional running workshops or training groups who might need help? Offer your help for a fee or commission.

Election support

This is very occasional work but pays quite well. Your local, state or national elections need staff to help manage voters on the day. You help people find their way to the ballot box, find pencils or fold the ballots. They search for staff through job agencies. I started as a teenager, but a lot of retirees and people on the pension do this for additional income.

Chocolates: Fundraising for a trip

When I was 16, I sold a lot of chocolate to help me pay to go on a water polo tour of New Zealand with my school. We were all encouraged to fundraise some of the cost of the trip, which was over $2000, and for our parents to pay the rest.

We did a few cake stalls, but then I had the idea to get some Cadbury fundraising chocolates. I ordered 40 boxes and formed a team to sell them. It was a hit, so I ordered another 120 boxes. Our lounge room was full of chocolate. I asked my parents to take it to work, my siblings took it to their schools and for months on end I carried a box to school with me every day. Some of my high school friends still associate me with the iconic Aussie chocolates, the Caramello Koalas and Freddo Frogs.

I also raised thousands of dollars for charities when I took on challenges overseas in later years. Note: you cannot do this for personal income, but you can do it for a community, school or workplace challenge to support your travel or other experience.

It's delicious but dangerous ... for your waistline.

Event volunteer

Volunteering at events is a great way to attend an event you can't afford. I've volunteered at comedy gigs, music festivals, conferences and more over the years to be a part of amazing events. I've volunteered for Business Chicks Australia at their breakfast, lunch and dinner events. I met the former Prime Minister of New Zealand, Dame Jacinda Ardern, and saw her speak in three cities by volunteering my time. Yes, I worked, but wow it was fabulous fun and such a lifetime highlight to meet such a remarkable world leader.

Some people frown upon this type of volunteering and insist that organizations should pay minimum rates. But volunteering at events is a common thing. Tony Robbins still does this; you can even visit his website to learn about crewing events. I call this type of income a value exchange, as I mentioned before.

Some experiences I had money couldn't buy. And I learn so much from the speakers and by seeing behind the scenes. I also have an amazing list of contacts from attending so many events. I invite and encourage many of my colleagues to join me volunteering at events for the rich experiences they are. Everyone who has joined has been grateful for the opportunity and loved being a part of it. They are also always surprised that they get to attend and get a meal too; that's part of the deal.

Are there events you'd love to see and could attend as a volunteer?

Passive income

This is the pinnacle of income earning for most business owners or online workers. To get paid while you sleep. There are many ways to be paid passively, but the two most common are commissions and affiliate marketing, which you will see below.

But passive income is anything but passive. As my amazing mentor Denise Duffield-Thomas says, "It's effortless, not effort none." Ha ha. Passive income requires effort to set up and to maintain, and it can come in so many forms.

One of the major forms we know about is multi-level marketing, which I have failed to make an income from. Nor would I recommend it to you. I've tried it and know my efforts are best used elsewhere.

Passive income is not getting money out of nowhere. It's the setup and the systems to receive money with little effort that makes it passive. You must do the work first to get the passive bit later.

Here are some occasions where earning income has felt passive to me:

- Getting asked for an invoice by one of my amazing photography partners, Meg Richards from Kruz Creations, while trekking Cradle Mountain in Tasmania because two people signed up for her photoshoots on my recommendation.

- Waking up to a client for my retreat. She saw one of my Instagram reels, connected on Instagram, exchanged a few direct messages with me, and then booked through the link and paid upfront for my Sri Lanka retreat in November 2024 while I slept.

- Someone bought my low-priced photoshoot guide from my website. I'd created it two years before I listed it on my website. I cried and felt as delighted by this sale as some of my thousand-dollar contracts. It wasn't about dollars. It was about the possibility of scaling my income and not being reliant on me being present to deliver.

- A coaching call booked online overnight, getting the money in my account a few days later and then delivering a one-hour gorgeous call with a client. Effort-less.

- Recognizing that my investment property was passive income. I got paid every two weeks for six years by my tenants.

Commissions

I earn commissions, as I mentioned, when I assist at events: either per attendee or a percentage of the income for the day. But I also earn commissions from business associates for referring clients to them. I recommend them, refer people to them, or promote them for an agreed commission of the sale. This was a boost to my income in 2023 when I was, at times, struggling to put out my own offers.

This only works when you love and respect the business you recommend. The client doesn't pay extra; it's just a way of sharing work. Lots of copywriters and graphic designers have a relationship like this where they refer work and receive a 10% referral fee.

This is also how I earn money through my travel partner, the New Delhi-based luxury travel company Indus Bound. We have an agreed commission rate for any Australian clients. I support these clients to plan their trip and answer any questions, I act as the intermediary ahead of confirming their trip. This has been an incredible source of income since 2017, with 2019 being my best earning year until last financial year. Then I saw my 2019 income matched in just six months.

How could you set up a commission arrangement with a business or brand you love?

Affiliate marketing

This is like commissions but is more formal. It's a strategy used by online course promoters. Most courses will say, once you have taken part, you can become an affiliate and earn money for promoting and recommending them when people buy using a unique code.

I've been an affiliate for courses, programs, retreats, tea, candles and even an amazing baby carrier product, Hackerlily HipSurfer Carrier. Hackerlily gives me a unique code that gives my audience 15% off, and I get a commission for anyone who buys. Need one? Head to hackerlily.com and use the code EMMALOVELL. Woo-hoo, everyone's a winner. Under Australian consumer law, you must disclose you are an affiliate or ambassador and that you get a financial reward for your recommendation. Check the rules where you live.

HOW ONE YEAR OF INCOME CAN STACK UP

So that was a lot. As you can see from the different roles I've taken on and my career progressing over the years, I've managed to find ways to increase my income. I now earn money a lot more easily than I did in my 20s. Here's all the ways I made income in 2024.

Monetary income

- Hosting retreats in Australia, India, Sri Lanka and selling upcoming retreats in Greece, Mongolia, the U.K. and Italy.
- Teaching people how to run their own profitable and fun retreats.
- Delivering courses on retreats and personal brand.
- Speaking.
- Emceeing.
- Coaching one-on-one: my hour of power.
- Selling PDF guides and workbooks through my website.
- Presenting webinars and masterclasses.
- Shares in companies.
- Investing in property: rental income and then profit from the sale.
- Mystery shopping.
- Commissions from the India travel company and my photoshoot partner.
- Earning affiliate commissions from colleagues for courses, events and retreats.
- Selling stuff from my house. Facebook Marketplace is a gem.
- Receiving an inheritance and gifts of money from my parents and loved ones (I am so fortunate and I track this abundance.)

Non-monetary income

- Entering competitions. I win SO much free stuff.
- Event volunteering.
- Free accommodation and hosting on some of my retreats in India, clients paying for my travel to co-host, and being offered family packages by hotels and operators who want us to promote their destinations.

If COVID-19 taught me anything, it was to have a diversified income. If you have only one job or income source and it goes, then what? When COVID-19 came along, I thought, "Yes, game time. I've been training for this. Put me in the ring." Because the roller coaster of my business journey had been preparing me for the unpredictable. I was ready to do whatever I needed to do to survive through a period of uncertainty. Actually, my business thrived because people had existential crises and needed personal branding coaching, which was my primary focus in the business. So, it was great. That is a joke. I am not here to profit off other people's challenges and misery. In all seriousness, though, it was such a time of need. People had a problem; I had the solutions. I love helping people to rediscover who they are and it was a terrific time.

Income learnings and reflections

I'm very proud of 2016-Emma who purchased a home on her own and sold it for a profit. If you asked me seven years ago if I could have a large sum of money in the bank, I didn't think I could. I have been working on my money "mindset." This involves recognizing where I have abundance in my life and where I am making money. I no longer think of my income as my salary. I don't have a salary. I have a lot of ways to bring in money.

You can change your mindset around money too. If you find 20 cents on the street, celebrate it. That's money. Money is money and you can attract more of it and make more of it.

When things feel tight, I turn to selling items around the house we no longer need. This shifts my money "energy" and brings in some income. In come. Not outgoings all the time. And if you ever feel you're above any of the work that I've mentioned in this chapter, remember: I have literally picked up dog poop multiple times throughout my life and career for money. And picking up dog poop pays really well.

Questions for reflection

1. What is your primary source of income now?

2. How many sources of income do you have? Write them all out.

3. What was your favorite way of making money over the years?

4. What was your least favorite way of making money?

5. What are some of the most creative ways you've ever made money?

6. Could you make some extra time each week to do just one activity I've suggested above (even taking online surveys) to bring in extra income?

7. Do you have any investments? And if not, how could you be investing?

8. What's your appetite for risk? High? Medium? Or low?

9. When did you last find money on the street, in your pocket, somewhere around the house? Now celebrate that.

10. In what ways are you being paid in non-monetary income, so that your cost of living or cost of leisure is reduced?

11. What was the last free thing you received?

12. Are you entering competitions, raffles or games? You got to be in it to win it, my friend.

Short and sweet

- You can make money in more than one way at once.

- To live a Bleisure life, diversify your income streams.

- There are many, many ways to make money.

- You can work for free for amazing experiences.

- I like to work as you can see because of the exciting opportunities I find.

- There are skills you have or items you own that can make you money

- Generating income is also about your money mindset. In my experience, focusing on gratitude and abundance brings more money into your life.

- There are easier ways to make money than working harder.

HOW I SAVED FOR A HOUSE IN SEVEN MONTHS

How do you buy a house in this day and age? It's so hard to enter the market.

Well, I managed to buy one back in 2016 after just seven months of saving. No, I didn't eat noodles and stay home the whole time. Yes, I had extra work, but with my business, side business and freelancing, this was the norm.

So, what was my top hack? Minimal to no living costs.

While I was saving, I was paid to live in other people's houses as a pet sitter. All my income went into the bank. Few expenses; maximum income. I promise I won't leave it there. Let's go back a few steps.

MY PARENTS PLANT THE SEED

I was 14 years old. My parents sat with a financial planner in our downstairs dining area talking about investment properties. Afterward, they said to me, "We wish we knew at your age what we know now."

They also shared with me a story of a 30-year-old woman who worked at McDonald's but had sufficient income to create a property portfolio of over $1 million. That sounded like a lot to me.

Soon after, they purchased their first investment property in Moreton Bay, Queensland. The seed was planted. That little seed became a vision and dream: to buy a house on my own and grow my property portfolio. I didn't set a date or time back then, which I now know is crucial when setting yourself big stretch goals.

STRETCH GOAL, NO PLAN

So I finished school, traveled the world and went to university all the while holding onto the dream. I didn't know when it would be possible. Although I thought about it, I had not planned or taken any real action apart from thinking: *When I have more money I can start saving.* Not particularly helpful. And slightly delusional.

I soon felt I was falling behind for not getting on the property ladder. Then in 2013, while living in Melbourne, I heard about the Tasmanian first home buyers grants. I thought, sure I can go live in Tasmania. The grant was a lot more than in New South Wales or Victoria and the property prices were lower. The dream seemed achievable.

I was pretty settled in Melbourne. I shared an apartment with a friend. I saw myself there for the foreseeable future ... but would work toward this house goal.

INSPIRED BY MY DAD, AGAIN, BUT NOT QUITE READY

In December 2013, I went to the U.K. to see family at the same time as my dad. We sat together in London Borough Market and he showed me photos of a townhouse he'd just bought in the beachside suburb of Coogee, Sydney. Now divorced from my mum (but on good terms) and living alone, he planned to move in shortly. My plan shifted in an instant.

"Hey Dad, can I move back to Sydney and live with you for a little while to save and buy my first house?"

Dad's new place had enough space for both of us and I knew he'd probably be happy for me to live there at low to no cost. The dream in an instant seemed believable and achievable.

So, in March 2014, I moved my life back to Sydney to save for a house. I know, right? Not a sentence you see often if you know the Sydney housing market. But with the housing market as it is today, getting help from your parents is really one of the only ways forward for young people. I'm forever grateful to my dad for helping me.

Still, I wasn't quite ready to give my all to the goal. I set off in April 2014 for a four-month trip around the world. It was one of my best examples of working and traveling—the true Bleisure life.

So, the dream went on hold ... Then, I met a guy in September 2014, a few weeks after returning (thanks Tinder). Now he's my husband. Hey, Mathew. He was also living with his parents and due to their travel schedule and my dad's, we had a very convenient living-at-home-but-having-space arrangement.

CONSIDER QUEENSLAND

A few weeks later, my property dream was rekindled. I went on a cycling trip to Cambodia and Vietnam as a tour manager and met a real estate agent, Ash. Little did I know we'd go on to be friends for nine years and he'd help me buy my first house.

You see the pattern here? This is why I love to travel. The expansion of the mind, the big picture thinking, the dreaming and then the serendipitous meetings in weird and wonderful places.

On the bus one day between cycling destinations, I told Ash about my property plans in Tasmania and about moving home to save and he said, "Well, have you ever thought about Queensland?"

No, I hadn't. Even though my parents had bought an investment property there I just was so fixated on Tasmania for its great grants, and being in a place I could potentially live for a year or two to make the first homebuyer's grant happen. I knew NSW was out of reach. My daydreaming hadn't stretched that far. Ash was a real estate agent in the regional area of Hervey Bay. He planted that seed again and opened my mind a little.

THE TIMER STARTS TICKING

I finally decided on a timeline: I would buy the house by the time I was 30. I was 27 at the time, so I had just under three years to make the dream a reality.

Time went by and the deadline drew closer, but I wasn't yet focused. I'm an all-or-nothing person, and when a vision becomes clear—like this book—I go hell-for-leather. I guess the desire wasn't strong enough yet.

Toward the end of 2015, my cousin Lauren was living in Australia on her own work and travel gap year. She knew I loved pets and knew Dad wasn't keen to take on the responsibility of looking after one while I traveled the world. She heard about some pet-sitting apps and suggested them to me. I loved the idea and signed up as a pet sitter on Pet Cloud.

Soon after, I got a gig over Christmas: $30 a day to visit a 12-year-old cat, 10 minutes up the road. He was adorable. It was easy and I had found a fun new revenue stream. And, as you read in the income chapter, I really took this idea and ran with it. I started my own pet-sitting business in 2016.

Thanks to the pet sitting, Mathew and I were then living rent free, and getting to test the whole living together thing. I also had multiple sitters working for me, and so also earned a commission from them. Our living costs were minimal, so all my business income—from pet sitting and Lovelly Communications—went to savings. My savings rapidly increased.

GET COMMITTED

But before I started the pet-sitting business, I got serious about the house. I had decided I could make it happen in 2016. I had to commit to making the vision come to life. To do that, I must see the goal with my own eyes. So, I got my butt to Hervey Bay.

In January 2016, Dad and I went up to visit Ash and his family and see the properties on offer. A big development push meant lots of new housing estates were popping up. We visited one and saw the types of homes I could buy.

I could buy a four-bedroom home for $329,000. You wouldn't get a hut for that in Sydney. I went into them and it was a standard home.

Tick. I did not want to be too emotionally attached to the investment. I looked at it through the eyes of local renters. It was near a school, a hospital and shops. Tick. Tick. Tick.

Then, the crucial step: getting an actual dollar figure to work toward. I had no idea about the real costs of buying a house. Would it be a 10% or 20% deposit? What would the stamp duty be? How much does the real estate agent take? I didn't know.

We met with a mortgage broker. I asked him if I were to buy that house, which was now the goal, and would be ready later in the year, then what is the bottom line, dollar figure I need in the bank.

His answer was $29,000 for a 10% deposit with mortgage insurance. So, my mission was set. Save $29,000 and buy my house as fast as I could.

A CLOUD WITH A SILVER LINING

Along comes June … I called the real estate agent, deflated, and told him, "I'm not going to make it." Because I'd worked hard but hadn't saved enough despite the pet sitting.

He said, "Well, here's the thing. The first homebuyers grant is set to increase to $20,000 and you would also be eligible for a $12,000 infrastructure grant." What? Not reaching my goal in time had benefited me! The universe was on my side.

Then, in the second half of 2016, I secured a six-month contract with World Vision Australia. That contract got my loan over the line. Sadly, banks in Australia do not look kindly upon sole traders, freelancers or business owners in general. I had to jump through a lot of hoops to prove my finances. It went down to the wire as to whether I could borrow enough.

The money saving had worked out though, and I had managed to save $42,000 from May to November 2016 while running my pet-sitting business, communications business and contracting.

With that amount, plus the grants, I was able to get the loan without mortgage insurance, which can be expensive. And funnily enough, in September 2016, Mathew got a job at Sea World Australia. I agreed to join him for the relocation to Queensland. We packed his car and drove up. We agreed he'd give it six months and see how it went. I planned to be with him as much as possible, but still spent a lot of time traveling for pet sits and work. I also still had the sweet setup of a room at my dad's where I could work from in Sydney when I needed to. It was quite a nomadic and flexible time.

HERVEY BAY BECOMES HOME

I had my new house as my primary residence for 15 months. I was still traveling a lot. In between visiting family and clients, overseas trips for work and play and pet sitting, "home" was a very loose term. From 2017, I approached a property manager to rent it out. This became an additional income stream (although it took me until mid-2023 to see it as such).

The term for my approach is "rent-vesting" (which I didn't know then). It's a great way to get into the market. You buy where you can afford and rent where you want to live. If you choose to rent the house out right away, you are not eligible for grants. But as I mentioned, I was willing to live anywhere for a year or two to qualify for the grant and get lower property prices. This is the beauty of having completely remote work through my own business—the ability to earn income anywhere from both the communications and pet-sitting businesses—and family, friends and a partner who were used to me jet-setting about.

DON'T SACRIFICE TOO MUCH

There are options for buying a home. It might take a bit of a sacrifice to get started but in the long run you'll have an incredible asset, whether you live in it or rent it out.

Although I worked for this and made sacrifices, my life wasn't very different.

- I didn't eat horrible cheap food at home every night.

- I didn't stop going out.
- I didn't stop traveling. Thanks to the pet sitting, I traveled more and got opportunities in other parts of the state and the country.

When I set the goal in January 2016 of buying the house, I was met with comments like, "Well now you're buying a house, you can't travel." But I knew that if I bought that house by cutting back, scrimping and just surviving, I would resent it. And maybe not achieve it.

I still got to live a life I loved, while working toward a big dream. In February 2016, Mathew and I went on our first international holiday. It was another dream of mine to travel with a partner. On our first ever chats on Tinder, I'd shared with "Scuba Diver Matt" a dream to learn how to dive and then visit the cenotes of Tulum. He said he'd teach me to dive. He did. On our overseas trip we went to California for an epic ski trip in Lake Tahoe, followed by a visit to one of my favorite destinations in the world, Tulum, Mexico. We dived in the cenotes (sinkholes), and I was so moved that I cried afterward.

Four years later, we stood by a cenote and got married. Dreams do come true. In the most magical and unexpected ways.

In 2024, I sold the house and pocketed close to $300,000 after all expenses and the loan payout. It's the largest sum of money I've ever achieved in a single transaction and have ever seen in my life.

GOAL SETTING WORKS

I was 29 years old when I bought the house. Buying it under 30 was the goal and I did it. Woo-hoo. Why? Because I set a goal to achieve it.

So, what big goal or dream do you have that you're not actively working toward? You can make a big, seemingly impossible goal happen if you put your mind to it. But you have got to decide and commit, then go after it.

And as Paulo Coelho wrote in his book *The Alchemist*: "When you want something, all the universe conspires in helping you to achieve it."

6

CHALLENGES

I would love to tell you everything always works out, but my life isn't all rainbows, roses and cruising around the world. (That said, I have just booked a seven-night cruise and I'm planning to do some publicity around this book on the ship. Ironic?)

In life, there'll be challenges thrown at you, whether business, personal, travel-related or something else (cough, COVID-19). This I can guarantee. Highlight reels on Instagram look sparkly, but they don't show behind the scenes. There have been many bumps in the road and dark nights of the soul. And times where I've questioned, "What the hell are you doing?" trying to make my Bleisure life work. It's not always been easy, but no great thing is.

I want to share what has gone wrong as I pursue the life I love, and the lessons and insights I have gained as a result. Choosing adventure and freedom has meant making decisions, sacrifices and sometimes failing. But would I choose the same path again instead of the tried and safe route?

A billion times, YES. Because it's been worth it.

In this chapter, I'll cover challenges I've faced, including:

- Personal debt and finance issues.
- Business debt and ways to improve finances.
- The global crisis of COVID-19.
- Pregnancy, birth and parenthood.
- Death, loss and grief.

I want to share how I've navigated these issues, showing how you can do so, too. While I love a roller-coaster ride, the dips and the peaks have sometimes been too dramatic. I'm trying to forge a cruisier ride ahead. (Again, cruises. A theme maybe?) Jokes aside, I'm trying to slow down, learn from experience and build myself a better foundation.

Challenges have taught me a lot. And yours will teach you too. But I'd like to help you manage your expectations better than I did, and soften the blows when difficulties arise. This is possible by adopting a new mindset to challenges and learning to anticipate the unexpected. We live and we learn. It's all just experience, right?

I'll never try to fool you and say you can work online, make tons of cash, travel the world and sip cocktails on tropical islands without a care in the world. That's not true and I'm here to show you another way. Nope, there'll be challenges all right, downs along with the ups, but you can do this. Let's get all the blah out of the way now, so you can plan for a sustainable Bleisure lifestyle.

PERSONAL DEBT AND FINANCE

Have you ever had debt?

- Credit card?
- Personal loan?
- Private loan to parents, family members or a friend?
- Mortgage?
- Car loan?

I've been in debt. Like *serious* debt. My first debt was a personal loan, taken out in 2008, for a car. I increased it for a semester of study abroad. And I had a credit card, too.

Fun fact: I was on the Australian TV show *60 Minutes* in an episode called "Generation Debt." Yep, really. You can Google it. I was still studying at the University of Technology Sydney. I thought my segment would highlight what university students went through. Instead, I looked like a spending and travel fiend (OK yes, the travel bit is true).

The host, Peter Overton, pointed to my personal loan balance and asked me, "So, this $12,500 is absolutely money well borrowed?" and I replied, "Definitely." That loan allowed me to go to Mexico and there I'd experienced the most pivotal six months of my life, studying and expanding my world.

In 2011, I moved to Melbourne just two years into my business with my personal loan and credit card debt and a couple of hundred in the bank. Burned out at the end of 2010, I'd stopped work for six weeks, and then taken a planned trip. My reserves had nearly run dry. I was struggling to get my mojo back and when a friend suggested moving to Melbourne, I did. I had no clients there, no prospects or leads, just an invitation and a suitcase.

Funnily enough, I wasn't scared. It felt like an adventure and somehow I knew I'd be OK.

Rebuilding mojo

A friend put me up when I first arrived and I began house cleaning, which helped me keep going those first few weeks. I felt good doing this simple work, too. Then I secured some work doing promotions and picked up clients by networking in small business communities. Before long, my business began to thrive in Melbourne.

But I still had that debt. And—let me be honest here—it had become crippling at times. It wasn't increasing, but it certainly wasn't decreasing either. I was paying high rates of interest, and just staying on top of it. If only I could wind back the clock and be kind to younger me. I'd help her to manage the situation and learn about putting money where it should go to best serve her.

The circuit breaker

In 2012, I knew I couldn't continue this way and made a solid commitment to myself to repay the loan. First, I had to stop spending and focus on paying my debt instead of paying interest. I canceled my credit card and asked the bank to roll the balance into my personal loan. The card had a 22% interest rate and the loan was 13%, so it made sense.

Then came one of the biggest sacrifices I've ever made: I said, "No" to attending a friend's wedding in the U.K. It was heartbreaking and I'm still sad about it today when the anniversary photos pop up on my socials. I was delighted for her and love her dearly, but I couldn't put myself under the financial strain of the return airfares and time off work.

Dreams of pursuing Bleisure were in their early days. I was very much stuck in work-work-work-then-play mode. My finances were feast or famine. I noticed how much I spent on traveling back to Sydney to see friends and family, let alone the U.K. I remember my aunt saying, "Oh, it would be nice to see you here again in London." That's what made me stop and think, "Wait. When do they all come and see me?" Not as often as I went to see them. While I enjoyed catching up, it wasn't helping me get on top of my debt.

So, I stayed home that time. I attended a conference, met my highest paying client to that point and, within months, I repaid my personal loan. Three months of focus, a few extra promotions jobs, committing to a high paying client, and I got that debt sorted. One less overseas trip led to a massive reduction in stress, a more sustainable approach to Bleisure, and took my business to the next level.

Lesson: sometimes you must make a sacrifice. Or more than one, even if it's for a short time. Focus on your goal, commit to it and you'll get there faster.

Make debt manageable

"Don't be afraid. Debt is easy to get into and much harder to get out of, but there are plenty of strategies you can use to make it manageable," writes Molly Benjamin, founder of Ladies Finance Club and author of *Girls Just Wanna Have Funds*. I wish I had this book back then.

After repaying that debt, I went on to buy an investment property. I proved to myself I could make debt manageable. The long-term gain has made that short-term challenge worthwhile, so sometimes a bit of focus is enough to change our circumstances.

Experiencing financial lows and finding ways out, often through many and diverse income streams, has shown me there's always another ace up my sleeve. That's the entrepreneurial way.

Now, I literally have an ace up my sleeve. An Ace of Spades tattoo on my left wrist honors and pays homage to my cousin Bill Hunter, a magician of more than 75 years. Currently 101, he resides in Roscoe, Illinois, U.S.A. and is one of my favorite people in the world, inspiring me with his approach to life. Perhaps he was one of my earliest inspirations for the Bleisure life.

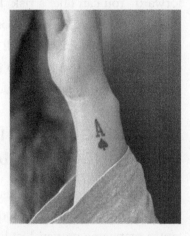

Travel is my lifeline, but also my Achilles' heel. In some ways, it's made me who I am and in other ways, my endless pursuit of travel has nearly broken me. Today, I won't travel at any cost, because I've done that, and it didn't work out well. But there've been times when choosing travel, and viewing it as an investment, has led to some of the greatest opportunities of my life.

I took a trip to India when I was 17 at the less-than-ideal time of four months before my final high school exams. A choice questioned by my 12th grade English teacher. Why then? Because my dad had a conference there for work and he was funding me tagging along.

That trip had no financial risk, and while the timing challenge was real, it turned out to be another one of the most pivotal decisions of my life. I've since returned 14 times and because of that first trip I now have a business partner in India. I host trips there and am paid a commission for organizing them. Because I traveled. I took the opportunity and the chance.

I'm not advocating for taking on massive debts. But now I understand my appetite for risk is quite high. I am willing to take risks for opportunities and to invest in myself. It's OK to have debt, then repay it. You need to take calculated risks sometimes to get you out of a bind, and they can lead to long-term success and opportunities.

It's OK to learn lessons, if you take heed and continue to move forward. You can take a risk, but plan to get yourself out of it. When I committed to and focused on paying back the debt and getting out of that cycle, life changed. I'll keep traveling and leaping at opportunities. I just don't want to do it with so much stress anymore. So, I'm working on my financial literacy, and more on that in the next section.

MANAGING MONEY IN BUSINESS AND IMPROVING FINANCIAL LITERACY

Of all the business challenges I've had, the biggest and hardest have involved money. Earning money, spending money and, most importantly, managing money. Just like personal finance, we don't get taught about business finance in a practical and applicable way. You must teach yourself.

Despite doing a business degree, including a finance subject, I didn't really learn about managing my business' money until 2021.

Have I had business debt? *Yes.*

Is it scary? *At times, yes.*

Is it crippling? *Some days.*

Is it impossible to get out of? *No.*

Again, it was when I got serious about numbers, writing them down in black and white, that I formulated a plan for getting out of business debt. Most importantly, I asked for help. You won't die from debt, even if some days you feel like you can't breathe or you're drowning. But you can avoid this stress with better money management. It's a skill and you can learn it as I have.

Separate personal and business money

The first 10 years of my business, I spent money when I had it. It was work, work, work and then I'd say, "Oh my gosh, I've got money. Let's go spend on the business and on fun things." Then the money ran out and I'd say, "Oh my gosh, I don't have money. Quick. Hustle." Sometimes I would go three months with no work. Other times, I had clients owing me many thousands and I could do nothing but wait. (Yes, I did chase up the invoices, but if they won't pay on time, you simply must wait it out or pursue debt collection).

During those times, I had to cover bills and life expenses from my personal reserves. Being a sole trader and freelancer, I didn't differentiate between business finance and personal finance, putting myself under considerable personal strain for the business.

I didn't recognize or acknowledge all my income like I do now (and have shared in Chapter 5). At times I felt low about not having any money, but I hadn't accounted for the money I had tied up in an asset, like my investment property. I didn't recognize the investment property as income, even though tenants paid me fortnightly.

I'm not encouraging debt or suggesting you enter stressful situations, but it's important to learn the big difference between personal risk and business risk. For example, when I moved to Melbourne in 2011, I had a personal loan, but my business was profitable. To me, though, money was money. It was all in one account.

Business money was my money. My money was business money.

Today, I try to keep my personal income and expenses separate from my business income and expenses. That means separate credit cards and bank accounts for my business. It still gets a bit mixed up, but I try to use the correct card or account for the correct income or expense.

Employ experts

I am not a financial expert or adviser, but I have built my financial literacy so that I can engage financial advisers and understand what they say. Please do not delay. Spend your time, energy and money (even if it's just buying a book) to build your financial literacy and understanding.

The banks won't help, as it's not in their best interests. You can forget credit card companies; their terms and conditions are a minefield of risk. And hard for mere mortals to understand.

Founder of Ladies Finance Club Molly Benjamin says, "Financial literacy is a critical component of women's empowerment. By providing the tools and resources women need to take control of their finances, we are helping them to build a more secure and independent future."

I agree. I had blocks about money. If nobody in your sphere talks about money, how do you learn about it? Seek out information and education. "Being good with money doesn't have anything to do with being a mathematics whiz," writes Molly. "It has a lot more to do with your mindset, beliefs and behaviors."

Molly's view was a revelation to me, but I have found it to be true. If you can get on top of your finances and have stability, structure and plans in place, everything else in business feels much easier.

It starts with wanting to understand money. I read books, do courses and hire financial coaches. I have an amazing accountant (after kissing many frogs). She helps me with tax planning. I have a bookkeeper to manage my accounts so I know where I'm at each month, and to give my accountant accurate and up-to-date figures.

Justine McLean is a respected mentor, speaker and financial educator with more than 30 years of experience and the author of *Become a Business Money Magnet*. I've hired Justine to help me price my offers, understand profitability and learn how to pay myself and contribute to superannuation. This might seem obvious, but many business owners do not do it.

"No matter who you are, or where you are on your business journey or what your relationship is with money, it's possible to understand your finances—the trick is not to get overwhelmed in the process," writes Justine.

My top tip for reducing financial overwhelm is to hire people who are specialists. Also, forgive your past self for what you didn't know. I've engaged a money mindset coach to support my husband and I in how to best use the money from the sale of our investment property. She'll help guide us on how to distribute the money, how we budget and plan together, and how to manage our household and personal finances.

Your money mindset matters

Money is important. And whether you love it or hate it, it's necessary in work and life. Build a better relationship with it, understand it, and make it work for you. For me, this has been one of the biggest challenges and greatest journeys. I know I could have been traveling and working with less stress in my earlier years had I known how to manage money better. For all things money mindset, Denise Duffield-Thomas is your go-to woman and her book *Chill and Prosper* is a must for those wanting to pursue the Bleisure life.

This focus on money mindset has allowed me to see I could have been saving, spending, investing, and managing any debt all at once. This was a key takeaway from Ramit Sethi in his wonderful book and podcast of the same name *I Will Teach You to Be Rich* and his Netflix show *How to Get Rich*. Ramit provides entertaining and helpful guides on money management.

THE GLOBAL CRISIS OF COVID-19

What would a book written in 2024 be without mentioning the COVID-19 pandemic? If you're sick to the back teeth of hearing about it, I don't blame you. However, I want to include some lessons from one of the most challenging periods of my career. It's an example of an unexpected business risk that we can all learn from.

And the challenge of COVID-19 was one few had predicted. In case you've picked up this book in the year 2048 and were not born when this global crisis occurred, let me bring you up to speed. In January 2020, a deadly virus called COVID-19 started to spread around the globe. By March 2020, many governments closed their countries' borders and enforced some form of "lockdown" on their citizens, asking them to remain in their homes to slow the spread of the virus. The world's activity paused. At the time of publishing this book, over 7 million people have died from COVID-19.

So many suffered through COVID-19 and still do. I don't intend to trivialize that. But COVID-19 did provide us with an almighty pause, time to reflect and an opportunity to realign with what mattered to us as individuals, communities, organizations and as a planet. Most of the world has gone back to life as it was before the pandemic, traveling and catching up with each other as we used to do. But many took the chance to "pivot" (one of the most popular words to emerge from that time) and head in a new direction.

The first few weeks of the pandemic freaked me out. As mentioned in Chapter 3, I was in Mexico in 2009 during a swine flu pandemic. From the way COVID-19 began, I guessed it would be much worse and more far-reaching than what happened in Mexico. I took a pause and gave myself space and permission to feel the enormity of what was happening. That helped me to take practical steps forward.

For me, COVID-19 tested all my past skills and experiences. I felt well prepared. My entrepreneurial approach to life, challenging the status quo, set me up to navigate the rollercoaster of COVID-19, especially when it came to how we work. I already worked from home, I was used to fluctuating income, and I was happy to do whatever work I needed to do. I found calm in the storm.

The lockdowns challenged my business. But I saw growth and enjoyed the pause from travel. I launched my podcast, *Lovelly Travels*, which was a lot of fun. I've since gone on to create two podcasts for my business and know these have led to thousands in sales and helped me with the content of this book.

When we're in them, challenges can seem insurmountable. But the pandemic taught me so much can come from a forced change. I had to slow down, pause and rest.

I hope you too were able to take some lessons from this time, because if challenges are nothing else, they're "AFGO." My dear friends Carolyn and Gillian shared this term. It means "another f*cking growth opportunity." I hope this acronym pops into your head at the next challenge you face, makes you giggle, and helps you identify what you might learn, in time, from the shitty position you find yourself in.

PREGNANCY, BIRTH AND PARENTHOOD

I'm not sure where to start with this section. For some, it will be confronting. For others, it might be comforting. For me, revisiting this time is healing.

I wanted to get pregnant. I wanted a child. I wanted a family with my darling husband and partner in life, Mathew. But I could not have imagined the terror and paralyzing state I found myself in the days after learning I was pregnant. Like nothing I'd ever experienced.

I was very unwell in those early days. At seven weeks pregnant, I had full-blown morning sickness and nausea throughout the day. I struggled to focus. I felt exhausted, and I had to do this for another 31 weeks? Would my business survive? I'd run my business for 12 years at that point. I loved it. And yes, I was one of those who referred to their business as their baby. So now, any thought I might not be able to continue it was devastating.

While I'm a positive person, in a crisis, my mind slides to the worst. I knew everything was going to change. I'd had lovely friends, colleagues and family members who shared honestly about the realities of parenthood. And it struck fear into me.

This book isn't about my pregnancy story, though I have written six chapters of a book titled *BS (Bullsh*t) On the Glow*, as we women have been sold a lie. If you'd like to read more, head to my blog at icallbsontheglow.com. I was told what pregnancy was meant to be like and how I should lean into the experience. I found it suffocating and pushed back hard. For me, pregnancy wasn't beautiful; it was exhausting and scary. I'm not quite sure which aspect is meant to be enjoyable? Because I didn't like one bit of it.

Now this might shock you because to see me with my darling son Finn, you'd never believe I felt this way. He is the light of my life and I'm in no way humble about him. He's adorable, a treasure and a joy. I love him endlessly. I was never concerned about loving him, not one bit. But I was aware of and prepared for post-natal depression because I have experienced depression and anxiety before. Fortunately, I did not get postnatal depression. I had all the support in place for myself in case that was the outcome, but it simply wasn't and I am thankful for that outcome.

Once I set a goal, my nature is to put all my energy into smashing it out. But when it comes to growing a human, you must surrender to the process. So, unless there's an emergency, there are 38 or so weeks of waiting patiently. You've read that I don't like following processes or doing things the traditional way. But this time, I had no choice.

Build support networks

If pregnancy is tough for you and even if it isn't, build your support networks. I'm grateful to those who calmed my nerves. They came in the form of women who'd gone before me and were not only making it work but thriving. I looked up to the mother of six and incredible entrepreneur Emma Isaacs, the founder of Business Chicks. I told myself, "If she can run a business, write books and inspire tens of thousands of women around the world while raising six children, then I can keep my business going and raise this one little boy."

Two other kind and amazing women who helped me during this time were Peace Mitchell and Katy Garner, the founders of AusMumpreneur Awards and The Women's Business Collective and editors of the book *The Women Changing the World*. During a seren-dipitous meeting at a retreat, they provided me with grace, inspiration and encouragement. With eight children between them and multiple successful businesses, they proved your business could grow after children. And, for the past 12 years, they have encouraged and celebrated thousands of Australian entrepreneurs, who are also mothers, to keep thriving and shining too. They gave me such hope and promise, and shared ways I could grow my business, thanks to this new phase of my life. And you know what? They were right. My income did drop in that first year but doubled in the second year. I make money with so much more ease and in far less time now, because I simply have less time to give to the business. I want to be with my son and my boundaries around him are firm. So, I am more efficient and more focused on building this Bleisure life for our family.

The lesson I took from all of this, dear reader—and what powerful learning it has been—was to surrender and let go. And I'm OK with being more flexible. I wasn't in the past. I would be stubborn to the detriment of myself and others. I love the movie *Frozen* and think the song "Let it Go" should become the mantra for all pregnant women. Since becoming a mother, I have canceled plans, postponed events and closed business offers. I ended a successful podcast because it no longer served me. It's OK to let go.

Sometimes, at work and in life, the greatest thing you can do is surrender. And I learned during a retreat practicing the Buddhist meditation Vipassana, "Accept reality as it is." That mantra guides me.

My son continues to be my teacher daily. I learn patience from and with him. I've learned to slow down and to do simple things. And whenever I forget and start getting stuck in my ways, I'm called to surrender and let go. His health, my health, and our happiness as a family are what matters.

You don't need to have a child to learn these lessons. There are many other situations, including pandemics, health challenges and financial events beyond your control, that can force you to let go and surrender. I hope this lesson is not quite so dramatic for you. As you read, take note of where you could surrender and let go a little to find and focus on what matters to you.

GRIEF, DEATH AND LOSS

And on that, there ain't no greater challenge than grief and loss. As I discussed in Chapter 4, a loved one can die at any time. It's hard to anticipate how you'll cope. But I can tell you one thing for sure: your priorities get crystal clear and quickly. Reiterating my kinesiologist Natalie Carden's kind words to me, "Grief clarifies living."

What matters most to you will strike like lightning, and you will no longer avoid what's most pressing. As you know, 2023 was a year of grief, death and loss for me. As challenging as it was, I'm now more motivated than ever to chase my big dreams. I cannot wait any longer. And this book is proof and product of that.

You don't always get one day, some day in the future. The time is now. Losing someone sucks. It is crap and awful and hard. But loss is part of life. Birth, death and taxes. We don't know when or how, but we know it will happen. Take what gifts these challenges can bring and, as my dear friend Paul says, "If we can't gain something from tragedy, then what the hell is it all for."

Review the challenges from your own life and see how you can transform them into your driving force for living a life you love. Now.

TIPS FOR OVERCOMING THE CHALLENGES YOU MAY FACE IN CREATING YOUR BLEISURE LIFE

- Have a plan.
- Diversify your income (Chapter 5).
- Call on your skills.
- Lean on your network and ask for help.
- Expect the unexpected.
- Let it go.

And as my friend Justine reminds me, "It's all right in the end and if it's not all right, it's not the end."

Questions for reflection

1. Are you taking risks in line with your risk appetite (see Chapter 5)?

2. Have you ever been in debt?

3. Did you get out of it?

4. How did you get out of it?

5. Could you get out of it again?

6. How can you plan in some buffers so that you don't have to run the feast-or-famine gauntlet?

7. How can you set up a system for yourself, where you're saving, paying off large debts, investing and spending all at once?

8. What support do you have in place if the shit does hit the fan and you find yourself in trouble? Name five people you could call. I bet you have 10.

9. What challenges have you overcome in your life? Put on a five-minute timer with music, just brain dump them all out.

10. Now look at all you've written down. Those experiences are proof of your resilience, and you can now plan to rise from a challenge when you need to.

Short and sweet

- Don't confuse the highlight reel with reality. Social media shows highlights, not struggles.

- Personal and business debt can happen, don't beat yourself up. Ask for help and make a plan to manage your money.

- Work on your financial literacy. Learn about money management and invest in financial education.

- Adopt an entrepreneurial mindset. To do great things and grow, you'll need to embrace risks and take opportunities.

- The Bleisure life is sustainable, but it won't come without its challenges. Choose what you're willing to work on and what feels too hard.

- Crises happen, pandemics happen, life and death happen. Expect the unexpected but know you can find a way through.

RAY PASTOORS
Working for a bigger
purpose

Ray Pastoors' innovative approach to integrating sustainability into digital marketing and his passion for travel make him an inspiring example of living the Bleisure life. Ray is the founder of True Green Hosting, a company that measures and offsets the carbon footprint of websites, promoting sustainability in the digital world. Ray also specializes in Google Analytics, helping businesses make the most of their online presence.

We first met during an Oxfam trek in Vietnam, where Ray's dedication to making a positive impact and his entrepreneurial spirit stood out. His curiosity with work has led him to undertake some fascinating roles in the last few years, not least of which was working as a flight attendant for Virgin Australia. I love how Ray sees work as experience, and although he likes to make money, it's about so much more for him than that. There's always a bigger purpose and it's inspiring.

How long have you been working in an entrepreneurial way?

I started very young, around seven, selling stickers for the Australian Koala Foundation. That experience sparked my interest in environmental sustainability, which continued into my career. I experimented with various content management systems like Joomla and WordPress, leading to the creation of an ethical digital marketing agency and eventually True Green Hosting.

Why do you love to travel?

Travel opens your eyes to different cultures and experiences, providing new perspectives. My first significant trip was a month-long Contiki Tour in the United States, which transformed my introverted nature and instilled a love for exploring the world.

How have you managed to include travel in your work?

I see travel as a reward for hard work. It's a form of self-care, allowing me to experience something new and different. Travel also triggers emotions and learning experiences, even when things go wrong.

You stopped working in your business and started working as a flight attendant. Why?

I had an epiphany. It was like I really wanted to do this kind of thing that I've put on my bucket list for such a long time. That thing was to be cabin crew for Virgin Australia. I kept running my business at the time, and just got to do more travel.

What would your advice be to someone looking to include more travel in their work or life?

Set clear goals for what you want to achieve with your travel. Whether it's a specific destination or a type of experience, knowing your purpose helps you integrate travel into your work. Business retreats and networking events are also great ways to mix leisure with professional growth.

Have you faced any challenges as a member of the LGBTQIA+ community while traveling?

Yes, certain regions are less inclusive, so it's important to research and be cautious. However, finding safe spaces and inclusive environments, like with our driver Anil in India, can make a huge difference. Creating signals of inclusivity, such as using rainbow flags on websites, also helps.

What is your dream destination to work in?

I've got a vision board on my screen which shows me the places that I want to get to. I'd love to see the Northern Lights or visit Antarctica. While these destinations might not be typical work locations, the idea of experiencing such unique environments is thrilling. Balancing work with these kinds of adventures would be amazing.

CONNECT WITH RAY

- Website: truegreen.au
- Instagram: @truegreenhosting
- Hear the full interview with Ray on my podcast, *The Emma Lovell Show.*

7

CHOICES

Sitting in Hawaii on a lounge chair by the pool, sipping on my pina colada and soaking in the sun, I declared, "OK, I'm off."

My two friends glared at me in horror. "Why?"

"I'm going back to the room to make some calls for work."

They protested my departure, shocked. How dare I leave such a scene? I was on holiday, right? I explained that three hours of work in the afternoon would pay for all my meals and activities that day. (I didn't add, "There's only so much lying around the pool I can do.") Despite their cries for me to stay, I committed to doing my work and off I went.

Back in the room, I sat with my laptop on the balcony and looked out over the beautiful beaches of Big Island, Hawaii. Our room was a few floors above the pool, so I now had a better view. I made calls and talked to clients, all while getting paid. Not a bad day at the office, wouldn't you agree?

In living the Bleisure life, weigh it up and decide what's important to you. Enjoying cocktails and a delicious meal at sunset is worth more to me than a few extra hours on a deckchair at the pool. Everything is a choice. Money versus time versus energy.

MAKE CHOICES

No, you can't have it all. Not ALL at once and not all the time. But you can have some of it, sometimes. You can travel the world and still make a living. Sounds like a dream, right? For me, this is reality. But as I've shared in earlier chapters and will detail here, it takes sacrifice. It may seem like fate handed me all of this on a silver platter, but I hope that I have shown that work, experience and connections have helped me make this possible. As well as the sacrifices I've chosen to make along the way.

Because travel is my passion, I've built my working life around it, running my business remotely with just my phone and my laptop as my "office." Whether you work for yourself or as an employee, there is flexibility with many roles now to work from anywhere. It's possible to go up to your boss and say, "Hey, I just want to take a long weekend. I'll still work while I'm away, but I'll just be in Adelaide Thursday and Friday." This means you're already there to enjoy the weekend, and at nights and early mornings you can enjoy the local area and change of scenery.

In my business, my clients always knew that I worked from different locations because I told them. But if you are thinking about running a business and you're not doing this yet, just working from home, please consider doing it differently. Look at more possibilities. Working from another state or another country. Or even just the local cafe for a change.

Of course, it's not all lying on beaches while tapping away at the laptop. It involves a lot of planning, discipline and sacrifices. But in my book (literally, ha ha, I'm writing it for you) the opportunities that working remotely offers far outweigh the challenges.

Financially, I have made choices that helped me to travel further and longer.

I'll ask myself:

- Do I want to buy this $100 dress? Or do I want to have an amazing dinner in Dubrovnik?

- Do I want to get this $200 handbag? Or do I want to spend an extra night on accommodation in Milan?
- Do I want to invest in this course for my business? Or go on a staycation on the Gold Coast with my family?
- Do I want to go on a girls' trip for a weekend? Or do I want to pay for flights to India?

Everything is a choice. I choose to travel every time and I choose bigger, bolder travel. As I wrote in an article for the ezine She Defined back in 2018 called, "How I run my business and travel the world," there are some downsides to the Bleisure dream. Yes, there are pitfalls to this blissful existence. I will not sell it all as sunshine and roses because it can be tough when you don't receive a salary with benefits. If you're running your own business, doing casual work, freelancing, or working as a sole trader, here are some things to consider before becoming a freelancing vagabond.

There is no holiday pay

Working year-round is not always possible and sometimes we need to switch off. However, with freelancing or running your own business (as a side business or full-time), you do so at your own expense. Have a stockpile of income to cover that period of no earning.

Superannuation is up to you

Contract or freelance work does not always include benefits like superannuation, insurance or pensions. If you're an employee and have an agreement where you can work remotely that's fantastic. They contribute for you. But if you're a business owner like me, then the only person contributing to your retirement is you.

When I was 25, I wasn't too fussed about superannuation (pension). Now, I'm dedicated and focusing on it a lot more. I'm working with my accountant on how best to make superannuation (pension) contributions and I set targets based on the average for my age group. Speak to a financial professional about how to contribute and focus on this early, and it will become a habit. One benefit of working in an employee role is the employer pays the superannuation (pension) on top of your wages and you don't have to worry about this. Something to think about.

Payment is not always swift

Unlike a regular employee salary, business owners and sole traders must invoice and await payment. Sometimes it can take 30 to 60 days or more to be paid. When traveling, this can be crippling. Keep this in mind and budget for the lag. That said, payment terms are up to you, so consider shortening your terms to seven or 14 days. You might even offer a price discount for upfront payment or shorter terms.

Income fluctuates

Some months you can have so much work you're turning it away. Other months you can have a complete dry spell. Have a buffer in your bank account to stabilize low periods. I recommend three months of living expenses.

This can also happen in a business where you sell products, even digital ones, or sell in advance, like my retreats. You have a lot of potential income with your products and offers, but you never know whether people will buy or how many will buy. So, income fluctuates and when planning to travel, this can be a challenge. You're banking on income to fund the travel and it may never come. Having the funds before you go is, of course, the best idea. But sometimes you have planned things way in advance. Have a backup plan, such as an overdraft or line of credit. Of course, you must manage it well. As you know, I've learnt some hard lessons there. (See Personal Debt in Chapter 6.)

Missing big events

Because of my travel, I've had to miss out on weddings, birthdays, big celebrations and events with friends, including mini getaways. But don't we all miss events from time to time? On my big four-month working trip traveling the world, I went to two weddings in the U.K.

Often, I base my travels around someone's big event. Another time, my husband and I traveled for seven weeks to seven different countries, starting with a wedding in the U.S. and finishing with a wedding in the U.K.

How you spend your time and who you spend it with is up to you, but this is a sacrifice you might need to make for the life you love. The party will go on without you, but you'll be having your own celebration. You do what YOU want.

Fund your travel to begin with

As you embrace the Bleisure life, you will rarely have to pay for your travel. For example, as a freelance travel writer, a publication might send you on an assignment and pay for your trip. Or there are sweet deals, such as being sent to a conference or event with all your expenses paid, then extending. That is great Bleisure.

But another way is to pay for yourself. Go on your trip and sell your story after. My clients don't always pay for my travel. I choose to travel at my expense and pick up the work when I get there. If you wait for someone to pay for your Bleisure life, you might wait a long while. If you want to go somewhere and try working differently, make that investment and back yourself. This is where making your income, planning and budgeting come in. If you get paid for the work you do for clients, or pick up some work once you get there, then it's worth paying for some flights and accommodation.

Don't be afraid to try Bleisure trips just because you have to spend your own money. You can work up to getting the ultimate Bleisure of being paid to travel and earning an income. In my book, it's worth it either way for the experiences and opportunities.

Blurred work-life balance

You might be better at boundaries than me, but the Bleisure life will require the blurring of work-life balance. Honestly, I just don't believe in work-life balance. I don't think your goal is to achieve a perfect

50:50 balance every time. Aiming for balance in this way will set you up to fail. Instead, aim for harmony. Everything ebbs and flows. Sometimes, one area of life requires more time than others. That's OK.

Bleisure blurs these lines. You don't leave your personality and sense of fun at the door when you work or have holidays and never bring work into your personal world. If you love what you do and you're passionate about it—as I am—work will be present in other areas of your life. Allow your work to eat in to some leisure time to have the experiences of a lifetime.

In 2012, I was in India, and it was the famous Holi festival, where they throw colored powders and dance on the streets. I had waited a long time to enjoy this celebration. But I had a deadline, an article that was due. And so, to get that money, I had to finish the article before I could play at the festival.

I knew that if I didn't finish it then, considering the time zone difference, I would not get the time to complete it. I'd stress out. So, I said to my lovely friends I was staying with, "You go down and celebrate Holi now and I'll join you soon." They felt disappointed but understood. I stayed upstairs in their apartment for two more hours to work on the article. And then I went down to play at the Holi festival. A small sacrifice to earn the income to keep me traveling.

Lack of sleep; time zones

Time zones are always going to be tricky when you work and travel. You may need to wake at 5 a.m. for a call or stay up until midnight to meet a deadline. Be prepared for inconvenient work hours. I've taken calls at 1 a.m. or 2 a.m., which would horrify some people (maybe even you), but then I slept till 10 a.m. And I got to be in a beautiful place for the rest of the day.

You get to decide what you're willing to sacrifice and for me, losing a little sleep here or there (not every day) is OK. I don't mind waking up in the middle of the night. I'm not a great sleeper anyway and after having a toddler, I am very used to it. For me, doing this is not an enormous sacrifice if it means earning an income, especially for high paying speaking gigs or important coaching calls.

I am not a morning person typically, but if I must get up at 4 a.m. to travel for work or to an amazing destination, you bet I can leap out of bed. I'm sure you're the same.

Be aware that with this lifestyle, you might have to adjust your sleep routine and adapt to the time zones. If you're not willing to do that, fine. You can find another way to make it work for you, but to me, it's worth it for the many incredible opportunities it has led to.

Instability in routine and structure

Echoing the point above, your routine will fluctuate with travel. Also, with taking on a variety of work and having a varied schedule. For some, it will be too big a sacrifice not to have a routine. But for anyone who has been on a holiday, especially an overseas one, you understand that your schedule and routine may change.

You may be more disciplined than I am and be able to get back into your stride in another country. But from knowing many freelancers, digital nomads and people with multiple revenue streams over the years, routine and set structure can be a challenge.

BELIEVE IN CHOICE

Now I'm sure you're sitting there saying: "Yeah, awesome, Emma. You go ahead. Travel and run your business. You've got other ways to make money. But I can't."

This is not true. It's a story in your head. Perhaps reading about all these sacrifices validates that inner critic telling you the Bleisure life is not for you. But hey, we covered alternate ways to make additional income in Chapter 5. I have more in Chapter 8, where I give you some travel hacks. You can make Bleisure work for you. It might just mean giving up three hours one day of your travel schedule so that you can have the rest of a fabulous trip. Are you willing to sacrifice three hours?

From London, England to Ibiza Island, Spain; from Toronto, Canada to the Indianapolis 500, Indiana; From Hawaii to the Bahamas. I enjoyed four months of incredible travel on a tiny budget because I made sacrifices, choices and worked while I went. You'll read more about how I did this. I know you have ways to make this happen, too.

In this book, I want to be honest with you and share the highs and the lows of the Bleisure path I've taken. I want to share what does not work, so you can forge a smoother path for yourself. Everything is a choice. You choose the sacrifices you're willing to make for the income and life you want to live. That might look different to mine. I just want you to see the possibilities available to you when you choose to make a minor sacrifice from time to time.

Questions for reflection

1. What sacrifices are you willing to make to travel more and up the leisure in your life?

2. Write three sacrifices you've already made to achieve your dreams.

3. Now write five things you're willing to change to increase the Bleisure in your life.

4. What are you not willing to give up?

5. What's more important to you: time or money?

6. How can you tweak or adapt something you're already doing to add in a bit more Bleisure? aka doing a few hours by the pool.

7. Looking at my examples, how can you make plans or strategies to minimize the sacrifices or find an alternate way? (And if you do, I would SO love to hear from you. Email me, emma@emmalovell.au)

Short and sweet

- A few hours of work while on your trip may cover your day's meals and activities, balancing leisure with earning an income.

- Swapping a poolside lounge for a balcony office with a stunning view means you can still work and enjoy the destination.

- Choosing a bit of work over endless relaxation allows for longer, more comfortable travel experiences.

- Every decision, whether it's about time, money or energy, affects your travel and leisure lifestyle. Prioritize what matters most to you.

- Communication is key. Letting your travel companions know your work plans helps manage their expectations and maintain harmony.

- Opting for experiences over "stuff" or short-term enjoyment will stretch your travel budget and give you many more adventures.

- Embrace remote work possibilities, whether you're a business owner or an employee, to open opportunities for Bleisure travel.

- Accepting the trade-offs of a Bleisure lifestyle, like irregular hours and variable income, makes the rewards even sweeter.

ELENA GABRIELLE
The life of a traveling comedian

There are few who can challenge me in the "who travels more" stakes, but I believe Elena Gabrielle is a worthy opponent. I would comfortably say she travels more than me. Her life as a global comedian traveling the world is fascinating and exciting.

Elena is an Australian-born, Berlin-based comedian. She captivates global audiences with her satirical take on modern relationships and uproarious musicality. Elena has performed in 65 countries, including over 700 shows with "Story Party Tour" and sold-out solo tours "DIRRTY" and "Addickted." Trained at NIDA (National Institute of Dramatic Art, Sydney), she combines her impressive singing range, from opera to rap, into her comedy.

Both being travelers, I understand what it takes for Elena to do this and regularly check in to see how she's doing. Visiting over 65 countries and performing nightly—sometimes moving on the day after arriving—can take its toll. But wow, does she do it in spectacular fashion.

I met Elena through promotion work, and then reunited through comedy festivals. I am immensely in awe of what she's achieved. I love being able to speak to someone who truly gets this Bleisure life and Elena really does.

What's your business or job?

I am a stand-up comedian and producer. I produce my own shows and travel the world performing comedy.

How long have you been working this way?

I've been performing since I finished university, so about 15 years now. However, I've been living this nomadic Bleisure lifestyle for about seven to eight years. Right now, I'm in Singapore and I'm jet-lagged. It's a constant state of always being on the move.

Why did you start?

I studied musical theater at NIDA and self-produced my own cabaret show when I was 19. My first international tour was to Indonesia with an Australian company when I was 21. That's when I realized I wanted to travel the world and perform. It took about eight or nine years to figure out exactly how to do it, but it's been my full-time gig since.

You love to travel and try to do it as much as you can. Why's that?

Traveling allows me to experience different cultures and meet new people. Performing in various countries gives me a unique perspective on the world and enriches my comedy.

How have you included travel in your work?

By producing my own shows and being flexible with my schedule, I can choose where and when I perform. This independence allows me to travel extensively and perform in different countries.

What sacrifices do you make to live this lifestyle?

There are many. I'm still single. I travel all the time, which has led to a couple of failed relationships. It's a very lonely lifestyle, especially traveling solo. Last year, my grandma passed away while I was touring and I couldn't cancel my shows. You sacrifice personal life, stability, and sometimes even your health. As a woman, there are additional concerns about safety and costs, like spending more on Ubers and hotels to ensure safety.

What would be your advice for someone to include more travel in their work or life?

Be persistent and adaptable. It's also important to network and find a supportive community. Start small and gradually expand your travels as you gain more experience and confidence.

Do you think the Bleisure life is possible and sustainable?

Yes, but it takes a lot of work, trust in yourself and your business. It's crucial to have savings before making the leap. The business plan has to be solid and it requires persistence. It's possible now more than ever, but it's not easy.

What's your dream destination to work in?

My dream is to do a show in New York City. I've performed in many major cities in the U.S. but never in New York. Another dream is to perform in Central and South America, like Brazil and Argentina. But New York is at the top of my list.

CONNECT WITH ELENA

- Website: elenagabrielle.com
- Instagram: @elenagabrielle
- Hear the full interview with Elena on my podcast, *The Emma Lovell Show*.

8

TRAVEL HACKS

Time for some fun. I know you came to this book for my travel hacks. So, let's jump in and explore some of my top travel hacks to save money and make the most of your travel experiences. You might not like all of them as much as I do, or perhaps they don't suit your stage of life. But there are many gems and if you take away one or two, I know you will increase the Bleisure in your life.

STAY WITH FRIENDS

Without staying with friends, I would simply not have traveled as much as I have over the past 19 years. On one occasion, I traveled for four months and paid for just 16 days of accommodation. See Chapter 9 for more on this story.

I am fortunate to have family members in the U.K., the U.S.A. and various states of Australia. And I've also made friends in many countries around the world. The more you travel, the more international friends you'll have.

Accept the kind hospitality of others and be willing to offer it in return when they travel to your home. This hack allowed me to have amazing experiences at a fraction of the cost. This is my No. 1 travel hack to reduce how much you spend and keep more of your income in your pocket.

Accept gifts

I once visited my cousin in America and returned with more money than I had when I left. Here's how. I paid for my flights. When I got there, I stayed with my grandmother's cousin, Magic Bill Hunter I mentioned a few chapters ago, then 95. Despite the generational gap and living in different countries, we are very close. As soon as I arrived, he told me he'd be giving me money every time I visited from then on. Such a kind and generous man. And I don't pay for anything while I'm there. He won't let me, and nor will his wonderful friends. They love to take me and my family out and host us. One of his friends even gave me some cash because he was worried about me not having any on me (I explained I had my card, but he was having none of it).

This isn't the norm, of course. Not everyone has generous relatives. It's an example of accepting the hospitality of family, friends, and even strangers who become friends. Be open and willing to accept gifts when someone offers.

See what the locals see

When a local person hosts you, you see much more of a city and everyday life. You experience the culture firsthand, and not just the tropes and stereotypes of the popular locations. This is one of my favorite things about traveling.

Now we have a child, we sometimes choose to stay in a hotel or Airbnb a bit more. We need our own space. But I still love to stay with friends and family to share that with Finn. It also means we get more support.

So, this is my top tip. When someone offers you a gift—a place to stay, a meal—accept their offer. People love to be generous. Because of the hospitality and generosity of friends, family and strangers, I have had experiences beyond my wildest dreams.

Be a great guest

When you live in someone else's space, you must respect their house and their way of living. It's on you to be a pleasant guest, make it work and keep getting those invites to come back. So here are a few tips on how you can be a great guest.

- Communicate your arrival and itinerary, allowing your host to plan their life around you.

- Bring a thank you present, even if it's just a little card or a block of chocolate. Saving money on accommodation is huge and this little gesture will go far.

- Have an end date for your stay. Don't overstay your welcome. Being clear is kind and it will help both of you be at ease knowing how long you plan to stay.

- Offer to help in the home. Often people like to host you and won't expect you to cook and clean, but always offer.

- Fit in with their plans and life. For you, it's a holiday; for them, life goes on. So, you need to adjust to their schedule.

- Invite them to join you on your adventures or outings. Again, they may be busy with day-to-day life, but it's nice to be invited. Someone once came to stay with me and brought a friend. I felt like I was their taxi for a week because they did not invite me to join in. Sometimes your host will have better ideas for you about what to see and do. At least ask and be open to sharing experiences with your host.

- Give them their time and space. Try to be discreet and have some time out or in your room, so you're both not in each other's space ALL day every day. It might mean just hanging in your room sometimes instead of the lounge room.

- Leave their home as you found it (or cleaner). Be tidy and neat in someone else's home and you will not disrupt their life too much.

These are some guidelines to consider. It depends how well you know your host and how comfortable you feel with them. When I stay with family and dear friends, it's very much *mi casa, su casa* or my home is your home. But if you do only one thing from the list above, communicate. Be clear with one another. That allows for a smooth and lovely stay. And a free or very cheap one.

HOUSE SIT OR PET SIT

Want your own space but don't want to stay in a hotel? Why not do a house sit, house swap or even pet sit? You could visit some amazing places domestically or internationally while someone else is having their holiday.

I covered this topic in the income chapter so won't repeat it here.

LOYALTY PROGRAMS AND FREQUENT FLYER POINTS

For the first 10 years of my Bleisure life, I wasn't loyal; I flew with the cheapest airline with the best deal. But I changed. And honestly—the frequent flyer points I gain from traveling with one airline mean I now travel in a much nicer way and save a lot of money. Choose an airline and stick to it for the points. This is now one of the top travel hacks I share with people who ask, "But how do you travel SO much?"

It was only after the COVID-19 restrictions ended, when I booked a few flights with Virgin Australia Airlines that earned me "silver status," I paid attention. I found some hacks, like booking at certain times to double my points and my status credits.

Work the system

I then looked into what I might have to do to get gold and platinum status. To gain the extra credit, I pooled my husband's account to mine. They honored his credits and I hit gold. After that, I needed just another 300 status credits to get to platinum. It was down to the wire. I had flights lined up, but calculated I was going to be short by about 30 credits. This calculation is an important part of reaching these levels, understanding how many credits you need and what flights will get you there. So, I canceled a flight, copped the cancellation fee and re-booked at a time that earned me double the status credits. That got me over the line and I've now been proudly platinum for two years and it is such a help.

Soon after, Mathew, Finn and I went to the U.S.A. We got double the points because of the platinum status; we earned 480 status credits as a family—over half what we needed to keep our platinum status for the next year—as well as earning 240,000 points to use in the future. I earned more points, kept my platinum status and got to use the United Airlines lounge on the way home, which was a milestone and a luxury after so many years of traveling on a budget. I felt so proud of how I managed my spending and channeled my efforts to secure this level of status for me and my family.

Enjoy the benefits

Status as a general concept might not be important to you. And it might seem elitist. I don't feel worried about status in life and am happy being approachable and relatable. But status in travel means many more perks than bragging rights and earning points. It means being able to move my flights forward and getting seats with extra room for no extra cost. It means access to the airport lounge, which means we don't buy the exorbitantly priced airport food. I also get extra luggage, fast boarding and inflight service, and first preference to rebook a canceled flight.

I now also get a higher status membership with a car rental company, which means we get an upgrade most times we book and extra service. We also got a premium level membership with a hotel of our choosing, and these stays will add to future benefits and savings for me and my family.

Share the love

After traveling for 19 years as an independent adult, I am proud of this status and share the benefits with my family. I've gifted gold status to my mother, who would never have been able to achieve that on her own. And I've gifted it to my husband too. My goal this year is to achieve platinum status again as quickly as possible (I have it until February 2025 and am over halfway to securing it again until February 2026). Then I will gift platinum status to my brother so he can travel and take his wife and son into the lounge, too.

For me, travel is a shared experience, and it's about sharing the perks with my loved ones. And sharing my wins and knowledge with others. Hence this book. I hope this section changes your mind about being loyal and channeling your efforts into a frequent flyer program. I also hope it doesn't take you 19 years to get the memo. Although granted, my earning capacity and spending power are much higher than they were 10 years ago.

I thank my dad for giving me a glimpse of what was possible when I traveled with him and we went into the airport lounges together. Again, it was so nice to share this experience and I felt inspired. Something to aim for. Thanks to his role as a chief executive officer in the organization he worked for, he traveled a lot. He received all the points from this trip because a business cannot hold points. So he had platinum status with Qantas for many years, earning lounge passes and flights at a heavily reduced rate, as well as discounted upgrades.

I could write an entire book on this topic. I have an episode of my podcast, *The Emma Lovell Show*, about it. Visit the online resources page at emmalovell.au/bleisurebook for how to access the show or search it on Spotify, iTunes and more. Yep, frequent flyers are a game changer.

Accrue points and status quickly

I'm using Virgin Australia as an example, which is part of the Star Alliance and now gives me access to Singapore Airlines, Etihad, Qatar, British Airways, United Airlines and more. Most airline rewards programs do have ways to accrue and earn more points through offers and shopping partners.

Notes on the Frequent Flyer lingo

Points: These are earned for flying or by spending at affiliated brands, they can be used toward seats on flights, hotels, airline fees, upgrades (to premium economy or business class) and more.

Status credits: These are accrued by flying and occasionally by purchasing items. You need status credits to increase your status tier with the airline. The higher your status, the more points you earn, meaning you get cheaper or free flights faster.

- Sign up to the airline partner program ASAP. Don't wait 10 years to maximize it.

- Sign up all family members if the airline offers to pool points. Choose one account of the person who flies the most to accrue the points and status.

- If you have a business, set up a business account. I'm a Velocity Frequent Flyer Member and I have a Virgin Australia Business Flyer account. I earn points for flying, as one does through your personal account, but I also earn points per dollar I spend through my business account. So if I fly to Sydney and the flight costs me $180, I'll earn 180 points for the business account and 750 points for the flight to my personal account (or whatever is the allocated points for that flight sector). It's essentially double dipping and as the business owner, ultimately all the points will come to me in the end. This is a simple way to earn more points for something you're already doing.

- Connect with a shopping loyalty program that earns points toward your frequent flyer program. For Virgin, it's Flybuys. Every time we shop at Coles, Kmart and Flybuys affiliated shops, we scan our card and get additional points. My husband keeps an eye on this and often sees deals announced with bonus points. The trick is to do your shopping at a partner store. We choose Coles over Woolworths, and Kmart over Big W for example. We are not buying extra stuff to get points; we buy what we need from stores or brands that give us points. On some purchases, you can also earn status credits which get you closer to rising up the tiers and earning more privileges at each level.

- Look at the offers on both Virgin Australia and Flybuys websites that tell you how to earn extra points. Check this regularly to make the most of your loyalty program. For example, 7-Eleven has a partnership with Virgin Australia. So, we buy our petrol there most of the time. At certain times they'll have deals to earn triple or even 10- times your points. Again, this is everyday spending, not buying anything extra or spending money needlessly.

- Consider credit cards. Not everyone is a fan of credit cards, and I am not a financial expert, as you will have seen in Chapter 6: Challenges. But I have found the way credit cards work best is when you work their system.

We only use credit cards that earn points for us. Most frequent flyer programs partner with a credit card and this is simply the fastest way to increase your points while doing something you already do—spending money. We put everything on the credit card and pay it off in full at the end of the month. Ideally, we don't overspend. That means we hold our cash in interest-earning savings accounts for as long as possible, and we earn points for every dollar we spend on the credit card. For example, through my business, I earn approximately 20,000 points per month. This equates to two free return flights from Sydney to the Gold Coast. Or I spread it out across three flights using some points and some cash (Points + Pay: the best way to utilize your points and get bang for your buck). We also earn about 2000 points on my husband's personal credit card and get another 1000-2000 points per month and status credits from Flybuys. Use your cards responsibly. This system doesn't work if you can't pay off the card when it's due. Please use responsibly and make yourself aware of their terms and conditions.

A little effort to set up can go a long way. Are you willing to change a few things to get these kinds of results?

LOOK FOR DEALS

Jump on deals and book early. You save big time if you pay attention and decide where you want to go. I know this can sound like a lot of organizing, but it's just an awareness thing. And once you build a habit of checking your favorite airline website, reading your Flybuys emails and scouting deals websites, you can stretch your budget and your travels a lot further.

Book early

Whether you are booking travel, accommodation or car rentals, book early. You'll get much better deals. Look for booking sites and companies that offer free cancellation up to the last minute. For hotels, I love using booking.com for this reason. We even canceled one booking and rebooked four days before our stay because the price per night dropped. I'm now Genius Level 3 on booking.com, their highest status tier, which gets even better deals and sometimes a 20% discount—again, learning to be loyal.

Find sales

In early 2024, I booked my family on a European cruise for August the same year. Because I booked during a sale, when kids travel free, I got it for almost half price, saving thousands. I got a week on the balcony area of the liner for all of us for the same price I'd paid for two nights on the balcony of another cruise. Seven nights for the price of two.

Go off-peak

If you don't have kids in school, don't travel during the school holidays. I've made this mistake a few times, not looking up the school holidays' dates and paying exorbitant ticket prices. If I'd planned, I could have avoided that. I've also accidentally traveled on Grand Final weekend for the Australian Football League which incurred big fees and big delays. If you can avoid any big dates like this, do.

Choose cheaper days

Some websites, like kayak.com, color the cheaper days to fly in green. Although I don't book through the app—I book directly with the airline or through my amazing travel agent—I always do my research here first. If my dates are flexible, then I choose the green day rather than the day I planned if it shows as orange (mid-priced) or red (top dollar). A quick scan can save you hundreds, or even thousands.

DO THE FREE STUFF

Travel experiences don't have to cost money. It is such a misconception that travel must be expensive, both to get to a place, and once you're in the place. Many destinations offer incredible travel experiences for free. You just have to look.

In Denver, Colorado, U.S.A., we discovered a free wildlife drive when I was looking up indoor play centers. We saw bison, eagles, coyotes and more. It was incredible, and they had a discovery center to learn about the animals. All free and right near the airport. Best way to kill time on our travel day. It became a highlight of our trip.

Some other ideas for free stuff include:

- Museums.
- Art galleries.
- Walking tours (you might donate at the end).
- Parks and nature reserves.

- Free breakfast at the hotel. Choose accommodation with this option.
- Buy-one-get-one-free meal and drink offers.
- Free pastry with coffee (quite common in Europe).
- Ferries.
- Trams and buses, e.g., in Melbourne, the tram route in the city center is free.
- Street performers (again a tip or donation), I love these in Covent Garden in London.
- Samples at markets. You don't have to buy anything. It's nice to do so, but you can always look.
- Botanical gardens.
- Libraries, some of the most beautiful buildings in the world, are free and they are an attraction in themselves.
- Walking around the city streets. Yes, walking is always free.
- Sunsets. I love the meme about this. Offset your expensive travels with something free: Cruise: $5000. Beautiful sunset: free. LOL.
- Sunrise. OK, you get the gist. Nature and looking at the sky are free.

HOSTEL DAYS

Hostels are the best for working out how to spend little to no money. They always know the way to stretch your dollars to the nth degree and get the most out of travels. And no, hostels are not just for backpackers and young people.

Hostels are a form of cheap accommodation found all over the world and there are people of all ages and stages who stay in them. Hostels have great locations and great rates for private rooms, including for families. They are attractive to backpackers because they travel on a budget and will share to save money.

You'll always be able to find a notice board or a wall of pamphlets in a hostel promoting activities. Budget conscious travelers tend to stay in hostels so this market is served well. They also may attract longer term visitors, so they might have job ads or ways to pick up income streams. You can join in activities such as pub crawls, game nights, walking tours and more. They are a gold mine for information on the cheap.

BE A DOSSER

My friend Lizzie from the U.K. was passing through Melbourne on her travels. She ended up staying with me for six months, paying us $A50 to cover bills and sleeping on the couch, or in mine or my housemate's room as we were often away at alternating times. She also helped clean the house and often cooked for us. Because of her contribution, we had our electricity and internet bills covered that entire period. In the U.K., Lizzie would be called "a dosser." It is very common to have someone stay on the couch in a shared house who contributes to the bills. You can be that person.

EVERYDAY STAYCATIONS WITH DISCOUNTS

Because Lizzie was a traveler in the city and Melbourne at the time was my home, she saw everything differently. She would visit the discount website, Groupon, and get us meal vouchers. She found out about great free events and regularly visited the hostels to get the lowdown on what was on offer.

She also did free trials at gyms. She did this a few times until she found a gym she gelled with and got a one-month pass, but she got at least four free weeks. And I did a trial week with her at one. Free fitness.

At the Gold Coast airport, you'll find a guide on what to see and do in the city with a bunch of vouchers inside. These are for tourists and you can find them in most cities.

I live on the Gold Coast. One day I picked them up for a friend and thought, "Why don't I do this every few months, since I come through the airport or go to hotels for events anyway." Now I pick up the what's-on guide and get great deals and discounts. We now know all the free events in our city and get to be tourists at home, enjoying all the perks of a holiday every day.

Does your town have a visitors' center, information center or brochures at the airport? Why not apply the traveler's mindset and check them out next time you need something to do?

I explore the traveler mindset more in Chapter 14.

Here are some questions to help you apply these hacks or come up with your own crafty ways to save money and still have incredible travel and leisure experiences.

Questions for reflection

1. Which of the travel hacks above did you like the most?

2. Which one can you apply in your life today?

3. Do you have a travel hack that I didn't mention?
   Write it down and pat yourself on the back. Or one better,
   send it to me and I'll share it on my podcast too:
   emma@emmalovell.au.

4. What's most important to you right now? Saving money,
   earning money, saving time or traveling? Work it out
   because this will help you decide which hacks to employ.

5. Ask your employer to let you work from home
   or elsewhere.

6. Are you a member of any frequent flyer programs,
   booking.com or other hotel websites, or car rental loyalty
   programs, where you can earn status credits and points
   for benefits?

7. Could you become loyal to one airline, one car rental
   company, or one hotel group to accrue points?

8. List five friends who live in lovely places you'd like to visit.

9. List some family members you could visit or who might help
   with your travels.

10. Can you do some house sitting or pet sitting? Is anyone
    you know going away soon so you could get a little
    holiday at a different home?

Short and sweet

Here's a little summary of my favorite travel hacks.

- Stay with friends. You can save money by accepting the generosity and hospitality of family, friends and even friends of friends.

- Be a great guest: be invited back (and save more money).

- House sit or pet sit. Receive free accommodation while house sitting or pet sitting both domestically and internationally. Use apps, websites or arrange through your own network.

- Join a frequent flyer program. Be loyal and pick a program. You can earn points doing your normal spending and use them for cheaper travel and some incredible benefits.

- Book early and off-peak. Save money by booking early, maximizing bonus credit offers and booking during off-peak times.

- Stay at hostels: great locations and rates and many are family friendly.

- Be a dosser: stay on someone's couch for a contribution to bills.

- Do free stuff. Travel doesn't have to cost you the earth. There are so many free activities to enjoy in all different travel destinations.

- Become a "staycationer." Don't leave the discounts to the tourists. Pick up great deals and discounts that venues and governments offer to tourists and use them.

9

WORK HACKS

We've covered off travel hacks, and now it's time to focus on work hacks. I'm going to share the ways I have worked over the years to get more travel and more leisure into my life. And you can do these, too. They help you increase your income, attract more work or be more effective and productive with the time you have. That's Bleisure.

These five big hacks are:

1. The power of networking.
2. Asking for what you want.
3. Outsourcing: hiring virtual assistants and executive assistants.
4. It takes a village.
5. Reward yourself.

THE POWER OF NETWORKING

Networking is, hands down, my greatest work hack. It has been pivotal in the growth of my business and enabled me to build connections around the world. I stay in most Asian countries for free thanks to my network of friends, family and colleagues. My parents are expert networkers and, as a child, introduced me to people and took me to events. I learned so much from them. And, of course, it's not just about what you know, but who you know.

I'm often asked why I attend so many events. It's because I belong to networks like Business Chicks, One Roof and AusMumpreneur. I also join masterminds and courses like Money Bootcamp with Denise Duffield-Thomas. Networking happens everywhere, from bars and events to workplaces and sports teams.

For me, networking is about creating genuine, long-term relationships, not just handing out business cards or making quick pitches. Emma Isaacs, founder of Business Chicks, emphasizes giving value first. She means give before you receive. Through networks like Business Chicks Australia, I've formed deep friendships that have supported me through many personal and professional challenges.

As the co-founder of AusMumpreneur, Peace Mitchell, says, networking is about reciprocity—supporting and helping each other. This give-and-take approach brings benefits both in business and personal life. Mixing business and pleasure is powerful and fun. Tina Tower, founder of Her Empire Builder and rainbow in human form, busts the myth that you can't be friends with your clients. Business is so much more fun when you engage regularly in networking and build genuine connections.

Top tips for networking

Join dedicated networking groups

Choose groups that offer both in-person and online meetups. Online networking has grown, but in-person interactions are still vital.

Take it offline

Don't rely solely on group events. Follow up with personal interactions to deepen relationships.

Give more than you get

Be generous and offer value to others. When you need help, your network will be there for you.

Diversify your networks

Join multiple groups for varied connections. But do be mindful to balance your involvement to avoid spreading yourself too thin.

Show up

Active participation is essential. Engage in the community to gain the true benefits of networking.

ASK AND YOU SHALL RECEIVE

My darling husband Mathew works in the aquarium section of theme park Sea World Australia. He believes, as do many of my friends and colleagues, that if you show up, do a good job and are loyal, somebody will recognize how great you are and give you promotions and opportunities.

Lovely one, I am sorry to say this is simply not true. It doesn't work like that. If you don't ask for what you want or are unclear about your direction, you will not get your heart's desire. Unfortunately, it's not always the best, most loyal, or most skilled person who gets an opportunity. It's the person who shouts the loudest. It's the person who puts themselves forward. It's the person who shows up and tells you, "Hey I'm awesome." Or says, "FIGJAM," which means "F*ck I'm good. Just ask me." They get the opportunities because they are there and they say, "Hey, what about me?"

This can feel disheartening and unfair. I see this happen in the workplace and in business. But I also say kudos to the person putting themselves forward. Of course, you must have the expertise and skills to do the job you want. And sometimes people don't. But kudos to them for giving it a go and saying, "Yep I want this and I'm going after it." That's how they get it.

Sometimes it's as simple as asking, "Why not me?"

How I became a blog ambassador

I learned this with the World Vision Australia Blog Ambassador Program. I noticed people on social media had become blog ambassadors and were doing these wonderful things because they were chosen. Well, I thought they were chosen. Actually, I discovered from an employee I cycled through Cambodia with on a charity challenge for the organization that they had applied. So, I wrote to World Vision Australia on Instagram and said, "How do I get involved?" They sent me back an application form. I filled it in and they accepted me. It was quite simple.

Had I not asked the question, I wouldn't have visited Uganda and met incredible lifelong friends, colleagues and clients. I also ended up with a role in the organization—a dream come true.

Skipper for hire

My husband landed a fun casual job on top of his full-time role that came through my love of networking. I was the emcee at an event on the Gold Coast called Women in Tourism. Before the event, I went around and met a few people. One of them was Tamara Briffa, who owns a beautiful little charter boat called "Rosie" for tours and private events. I said, "Oh wow, my husband has just got his skipper (boat driving) ticket, and he wants to drive more boats."

Offhandedly, I added, "If you ever need more boat drivers, he's available."

She said, "Actually, I'm pregnant, and we will need a skipper because my husband and I will both be looking after the baby." We exchanged details. It turned out the woman beside her at the breakfast also worked for a charter agency and they needed skippers, too. By simply being interested, listening to these women and being clear, the chat turned into a role. My husband now earns extra money driving a gorgeous little boat at sunset around the Broadwater near our home. Not a bad little gig, if you ask me.

And then it happened again. There's a common thread here. Remember: ask and you shall receive. Just a few months before this book came out, Mathew and I were out in Surfers Paradise, the main tourist hub of the Gold Coast, and our son Finn was playing near the

AquaDuck shop. The AquaDuck is a bus that becomes a boat and takes tourists around the city and then onto the Broadwater. While Finn played, I asked the attendant, "Hey, what sort of license do you need to drive your boats?" He said, "You need a bus license as well as a boat license."

I said, "Oh well my husband has his MED5 skipper ticket, and he does a bit of casual boat driving. Thank you for letting me know."

Later that day, my husband took my son back into the shop and the attendant said, "Was it your wife who came in earlier and told us you had a skipper ticket? We've just purchased another company in another suburb of the Gold Coast and they need a skipper. Would you mind if we took your details and got in contact?"

Asking a simple question has led to additional income for my husband doing something that he loves—driving boats. Moral of the story: if you don't ask, you don't get. When you ask, you receive.

Take a moment to reflect: when did you last ask for what you wanted?

Have you asked for that promotion?

Are you putting yourself forward for that opportunity?

Are you saying, "Hey I'm available for work?"

The day I came back from four months' maternity leave, I put the word out that I was ready for work on LinkedIn. A client wrote that day and said, "Great. You're back. Can we book a strategy call?" I secured a sale from one social media post just by sharing my availability.

If you don't ask, if you don't shout out loud about what you want, then you simply will not get it. So how are you going to ask out loud to get more opportunities?

THE POWER OF OUTSOURCING

How do I do it all? I don't. I simply don't. I outsource some of my work to people who can do it faster and better than I can. I have contracts with assistants with specialist skills and I will explain how it all works. For now, let's bust a few myths.

Outsourcing doesn't mean relinquishing control and responsibility. As the business owner, you decide. It simply means being more effective with your time. You have people on your team, but that doesn't mean you do nothing. There's still plenty of work you must do; you must oversee administration, check details and lead your team. But you can save a lot of time.

A cautionary tale

As I mentioned earlier, my nephew had been diagnosed with a terminal illness in 2023 and I struggled with the stress and grief of this. I wasn't overseeing my assistants' work enough and let them lead the way. One day, I realized I was no longer in control of my business. I wasn't happy with the direction I had allowed them to take. Thinking back, I feel compassion for my situation. But I also take responsibility for not stepping in and taking control.

I would have been better off stopping work for a while than allowing my business to veer off course. It took months to get it back on track and build back trust. I found the most incredible person, Cat Dunn, my online business manager at the time, to breathe life back into me and into my business. With her help, I realigned my team. I don't think my business would have survived without her help. I will forever be grateful to Cat for that help.

Consistent help

One of my biggest hacks these days is to have consistent help and systems and processes. Early in my business, I outsourced. I've had subcontractors and assistants for years. But I didn't have the support consistently enough. I recruited help the feast-or-famine way. When I was busy, I'd get help. As soon as my work dropped off and income slowed, I would cut back to just me. As soon as it got busy again, I had to train a new assistant from scratch. Also, I wasn't documenting the processes. So, when somebody left, I had to start all over again. In 2019, I recognized the importance of consistency and contracted a virtual assistant (meaning my assistant worked online). I started with just a few hours a week.

Now, this might seem like it's only an option if you run your own business, but people have assistants in their personal life too. You could have a housekeeper, a cleaner or a nanny. People employ assistants to help them keep on track with life's demands. There are even people who will organize your closet, as you will know if you watch the TV show *The Home Edit*, which I was obsessed with for a while. A closet organizer is one of my next hires. I want someone to sort out my wardrobe and to help organize our entire home for better storage. This will be a huge support for my focus and remove a lot of the home mental load.

Hiring assistants

But let's go back to virtual assistants (VAs) and how they can help you in business or your side business. Hiring a VA can be the difference between success and failure. Had I hired virtual assistants, my pet sitting business (see Chapter 5) might still run today. When I closed that business, I was at a crossroads. I needed to invest heavily to grow the business and needed an assistant because the administration was sucking up my time and energy. I wanted more time for my communications business. So, without knowing about virtual assistants, I decided not to be a pet sitting mogul. I closed the business. Not a failure, but a pity.

Your options

You can hire virtual assistants who work in Australia, your home country, or offshore in places such as the Philippines. I have a combination of both. I have an incredible executive assistant (who works closely with me managing my diary, sorting my inbox, managing other contractors and generally being an admin superstar) here in Australia. Her name is Amber Field from Operation Amber. And I have two amazing VAs through the VA agency Kaya Services, who I've been working with for three years.

The benefit of working with a VA agency is that they hire the VAs and you hire the agency. If I ever have an issue with a team member or need different skills, I ask the agency and they allocate me someone new. My former team member then works for another agency client.

Get processes in place

My first VAs worked just two hours a week for me. I slowly increased their hours to three, then five and then 10. I hired the incredible VA Leah Selfe, The Productivity Queen, to help get my processes and systems in order. Leah helped me launch my second podcast, *Live & Love Your Brand*, and my first ever online course, "How to Live and Love Your Brand." She also wrangled me during the most hectic time of my life: the first year of running my business with my darling baby boy, Finn.

Because I now had documented processes and systems in place, I could bring on more VAs and free up more of my time. Leah also helped me to manage the VAs because sometimes that's where I fall over. Managing people is a skill you will need to learn, but it can be time-consuming and at that stage of business, I needed that support.

People sometimes say VAs don't work. That's because they do not train them or set up systems for them. Offshore VAs will do many rote tasks for you. Be ready to provide more initial guidance. Once they understand the task, they take it and they run with it, and they are effective beyond belief.

Be the CEO

I simply could not produce the content and volume of work and keep my business running without my assistants now. At this present moment, I have my EA in Australia for eight hours per week and I have my offshore VAs for 10 hours per week. That's 18 extra hours per week I have in my business and life. I still drive the business vision and maintain control over my business. But there are a lot of tasks that are unnecessary for me to do.

There's a wonderful book about this called *The E Myth: Why Most Small Businesses Don't Work and What to Do About It* by Michael Gerber. He explains how entrepreneurs fall into the trap of trying to be the technician, the manager and the CEO. You start as the technician, but as your business grows, you shift up the levels. At each level, you get the support to do what you can no longer do as the manager and the technician.

Today, with my EA operating as the manager and my VAs operating as technicians, I can stay in my lane: delivering the most high-end services, creating ideas, building relationships, speaking, hosting the podcast, writing this book and driving the business forward. AKA, doing what I love. This has contributed massively to how I live my Bleisure life.

My VAs do the following tasks for me:

- Podcast editing.
- Transcribing of the podcast.
- Video grabs for promotion.
- Show notes for the podcast.
- Publishing the podcast.
- Social media content planning.
- Reels creation.
- Canva tile creation.
- PDF creation.
- Google Drive filing.
- Google Drive organization.
- Image management.
- Website edits.
- EDM (newsletter) creation.
- LinkedIn newsletter creation.
- Article creation.
- Scheduling of social media.
- Stories posting.

You may not recognize what all these tasks are, but they are all now essential to my business. They do all of this with my guidance and the words and messaging come from me. But putting it together, creating visuals and getting it up and out on time, that's them. I cannot speak more highly of my team and the support of VAs.

I have no issue with offshoring—contracting people who live overseas. My business is global. I enjoy supporting the global economy. My VA agency, Kaya Services, treats their staff with the utmost respect and they have an incredible team culture. I used to see assistants as subcontractors and not part of my business. Working with them has helped me to see my VAs and my EA as my team.

I'm now so proud to say I have a team. My team helped me to travel even more in these past few years. I know day-to-day tasks can go on without me.

Recently, I had one of the most blissful days of work where I realized my team was truly helping me to grow. I could see the possibility and the opportunity for so much more in the future. I was hosting a retreat day in Sydney, where I teach people how to run profitable retreats. We were at a fabulous hotel, the Manly Pacific, enjoying a luxurious experience while helping these incredible businesswomen to bring more profit, fun and travel into their business through retreats. I didn't worry at all that day about what I had to do in my business. I could be completely present with my clients.

I have long worried when I run these retreats that normal business tasks, such as social media, might fail because I'm not available that day. However, at 5:30 p.m. while having a drink to celebrate our successful retreat day together, I checked my messages. I could see they had been busy posting on my social channels and clearing my email inbox. They had responded to everyone and filed my emails appropriately. My calendar was up-to-date, and I hadn't missed a thing.

My EA and my VAs teamed up and sent my weekly newsletter, as well as publishing a podcast episode and my social posts on time. Tears filled my eyes, and I felt so proud of what I had built and how this team felt empowered to take actions on my behalf. My business had continued to run smoothly and effortlessly whilst I could support my clients 100% and enjoy my day with them.

I thank my team profusely for what they were allowing me to do in my business and in my life. I'm so excited to see where this takes us. And I know in my next book, I'll have even more examples of how this works.

Of course, there are also days where it doesn't work so well. We have our challenges and feel frustrated with one another. Nevertheless, I am so grateful for my team. If I can give you one piece of advice, please explore the world of VAs. Engage the expertise of these skilled people to help you grow your business. You are also helping them to find financial freedom and build a life they love, too.

IT TAKES A VILLAGE

Whether you work in a job, run a business, have a family or are single, it takes a village to reach success. As an African proverb goes, "If you want to go fast, go alone. If you want to go far, go together." There are so many people I want to thank for their support over the years in my business and life that I have created a chapter for my acknowledgments. I simply cannot run the business I run and live the life I live without their support: physically, emotionally and mentally.

Your business village

For example, here is a list of the people who help me in my business:

- Executive assistant.
- Virtual assistant (VA).
- Online business manager.
- Graphic designer.
- Photographer.
- Videographer.
- Speaking coach.
- Mentors.
- Business coach.
- Networking groups (e.g., Business Chicks, One Roof).

- Conferences (e.g., The Content Byte, Movers & Breakers).
- Bookkeeper.
- Accountant.
- Pricing coach.
- Money mindset coach.

I've probably missed some, but that's a lot, right? That's what you need to run a successful business. It might not be all of these at once. But you do need help and support in areas that aren't your zone of genius or you don't have time for.

Your personal village

And here's the personal support in my life.

- Cleaner.
- Occasional food delivery services.
- Physio.
- Virtual personal trainer.
- Psychic.
- Psychologist.
- Kinesiology.
- Naturopath.
- Doctors.
- Parents.
- In-laws.
- Friends.
- Colleagues.
- Babysitters.
- Other family members.

This list might seem ridiculous. Yes, I've taken it to the nth degree, but I want to show you: I do not do this alone. So many people helped me in my business and my life. If you are not asking for support, you cannot go far. You will burn out. You will not achieve what you want to achieve or live a life you love.

Success is something we share. As a community, we come together. Humans are tribal at heart and need connection as author Johann Hari explains in his wonderful book *Lost Connections: Uncovering the Real Causes of Depression—and the Unexpected Solutions*.

You can't show up for work and be your best without the support of other people. Celebrities are a great example. Look at someone like Canadian singer Celine Dion. Her gift is to perform in front of thousands of people. Her role is to entertain us and create music we love. The list of people it would take to get her on the stage and keep her performing at her best every day would be insane. Look at American songwriter Taylor Swift. For her Eras tour of the world, city administrations had to change infrastructure and transport so her fans would get to her concerts and back safely.

Whether it's at work or at home, get the support you need to show up to work fresh and do your job well. That way, you can be "the golden goose," as my friend Denise says. To make the money, you need a support system—a village—in place. You need to be taken care of and supported to perform at your best. This is how you get to live a life you love.

MY REWARD SYSTEM

My clients love the way I reward myself. I didn't realize my rewards system was anything special. I thought everyone had a system to treat themselves until I was sitting around the breakfast table at one of my retreats and shared my rewards system. What fascinated my clients was how I set a goal and attached a reward to it. I've done this for years. And of course, a lot of my rewards involve travel.

My reward system is quite simple. When I see an object or experience I want—a swimsuit, a pair of earrings, a retreat or even a car—I add it to a list on my phone. I use the notes app mostly, but I also have an email folder called "rewards" and a spreadsheet for when I'm feeling more organized.

Then I write what I must do to get that reward. For example, "When I get my next big client, I can book the retreat." I add the specific link to the object of my desire. Or "When my next retreat client signs on, my reward will be a swimsuit from Indigenous Australian-led brand Liandra." I add the link to the exact garment I want. I'm more motivated to go after that client for the reward than just for more money. In the past, paying off debt has motivated me to work hard, but these days I'm more driven by rewards. And, if it's travel, I'll double down.

You can use this in goal setting, too. And if the trip you want seems out of reach and daunting because of the money involved, break it down into smaller goals. Let's say you want to take your family to Bali on the school holidays. You estimate it will cost about $10,000. Break this trip down and look at how to work for each bit of the total cost.

For example:

Car hire:	$800
Hotels:	$3000
Flights:	$4000
Activities:	$850
Spending money:	$1350

Now identify each sale you need to make to reach your target. Ta-da. A goals list for income to help pay for your trip. For me that might be one retreat client, one VIP mentoring day, four coaching hours, and selling three unused possessions on eBay. I wrote out a goal list like this for a family trip to Europe and had so much fun crossing off the items. Or you could draw yourself a little thermometer on the wall, marking off your goal amounts as you hit them. Whatever is going to help you stay focused on each target.

The secret of specifics

Your goals must be specific. Not, "I want more clients" or, "I want more money" or, "I want that thing, but I can't get it." General goals don't help. Have a goal and set a specific reward against it. Be clear, and the universe will help you get there. Or, if you're not into manifesting like me, your goals will make you more focused and motivated to do the work you need to do to hit them.

In early 2018, I set myself a goal of making $30,000 in three months to go on a big seven-week trip. I made $32,000. I worked so diligently in those months because I knew I had that deadline and the goal to look forward to. I had also written out everything I needed to live in those few months—expenses, possible hiccups (buffer)—as well as how much I needed for the trip. My goal was clear.

Another lovely example was a time I set myself the reward of buying a pair of signature pineapple earrings from the fabulous jeweler Alex Tempany. I wrote to her—she is a colleague and friend— to explain that when I got my next coaching client, I'd buy myself a pair of her earrings. A few months later, I texted and said, "I got the client. Now I'm off to buy myself those earrings."

She wrote back, "Yay, you. But I must tell you something. And I'm allowed to share a secret. Your mum bought those earrings already for you for Christmas."

Ha ha. I had manifested them without even realizing it. I replied, "Oh well, I'll just have to buy myself some hoops then." And that was a win for me, because they were less than I intended to spend, so I kept the difference. Win-win!

The lesson here: reward yourself for your work. You can't just work, work, work and one day play. Whether it's buying a piece of jewelry, a dinner out, a weekend away, or just giving yourself half a day off. And when you reward yourself, savor the moment by acknowledging, "Hey, I did something good, and I can do this again and have more of this feeling." It's called positive behavioral therapy, and it's used to train animals. If it works for your dog, or a sun bear at Taronga Zoo, it can work for you. So, go on; treat yourself.

Questions for reflection

1. What work hacks do you have in your own life? Write them down. Now you've got your own list of tips and tricks.

2. Which of my work hacks could you apply to your life now?

3. Which networking groups are you already a part of?

4. Which networking groups or organizations or events could you attend soon? Write three.

5. Are you asking for what you want? It's a simple yes or no.

6. How can you ask for what you want?

7. Set a goal and work out how you can put yourself forward. Ask to get the opportunities you want.

8. What are you outsourcing in your personal life?

9. What are you outsourcing in your work or business?

10. Write three things that you do not need to do. It could be gardening, cleaning, transcribing.

11. Do you have virtual assistants?

12. What tasks do they do?

13. Write five more things an assistant could help you with.

14. What support do you have in your work and life for times when things are challenging?

15. Practice gratitude. Reach out and thank your village today.

16. How are you asking for help?

17. Are you celebrating yourself?

18. What rewards can you write, at least five, to motivate you toward your goals?

Short and sweet

Living a life you love is about finding hacks or support, so you can share some of the work, and focus on what you do best.

- Leverage the power of networking.

- Ask for what you want.

- Outsource. Specifically, hire virtual assistants and executive assistants.

- It takes a village to raise a human, to run a business, to support you. Ask for help.

- Reward yourself with incentives, goals and treats along the way to help you keep going.

DANIELLE PHYLAND
Balancing full-time work and travel

Danielle is a passionate tourism professional with over 20 years' experience. She's not just a thinker but a doer, always coming up with creative ideas to boost businesses and destinations through her knack for communication, marketing, and promotion. Off the clock, her love for travel still burns bright. She has traveled to all seven continents and over 65 countries. Now, she's turned her adventures into stories as a travel writer, sharing her escapades in locations from local gems to far-off lands.

Can you start by describing your job or business?

Absolutely. I am a Melbourne-based travel writer, and I've been writing for six years. I also have a full-time job in the tourism industry, where I write strategic plans for businesses and government. My number one passion is travel, and I share my stories with my community at [my website] the Adventures of Poss and Ruby.

How long have you been working this way?

My journey in travel spans more than 20 years. I used to take my annual leave from my full-time government job and go on Contiki Tours as a guide. I got the experience of the holiday and got paid for it.

The travel writing was very much on the side, but I rebuilt and rebranded my website during COVID-19, leading to more opportunities. I've written for major publications like *The Herald Sun* and have been featured on multiple podcasts and websites.

How do you balance work and travel?

I work full time but have adapted that to my travel lifestyle. I've negotiated a nine-day fortnight, allowing me to travel more frequently.

I've purchased additional leave so I could make bigger trips. My ritual is I do a big trip a year, which is usually a month-long jaunt to a bucket list destination.

What does Bleisure look like to you?

Making the most of my nine-day fortnight. I can have long weekends often but I also squeeze in the travel wherever I can.

I also do silly things like go to New Zealand for a long weekend. It's quite an easy thing for me to jump on a plane for three hours and visit friends or have adventures in New Zealand or other nearby countries and continents.

Through my travel writing, I get experiences I might not otherwise have had the opportunity to have.

What would you tell someone who would like to embrace the Bleisure lifestyle but works full time?

Be clear about your priorities and be willing to make sacrifices. For me, travel is a priority. Always look for ways to blend work and travel, whether through negotiating leave or finding roles that incorporate travel.

Learn to pitch your ideas and build relationships in the industry. This has been crucial for securing travel opportunities.

What's planned for the future of your Bleisure lifestyle?

I aim to continue traveling and writing, exploring new destinations, and sharing my experiences. I hope to further develop my travel writing platform and engage more with my audience.

My mission is to inspire others to explore the world and see the beauty of different cultures and experiences. I want to show that travel is accessible and can be integrated into any lifestyle.

What would you change about how you've juggled work and travel?

I don't have many regrets, but if I could, I might have started travel writing earlier. However, I'm grateful for the journey and the experiences I've had along the way.

What does living a life you love now look like?

Right now, I have traveled to all the continents in the world. I factor travel into almost every day. If the sun's out and there's a winery with a band or an exhibition that I want to see, I'm out there. I'm living the life I love every day.

CONNECT WITH DANIELLE

- Website: possandruby.com.au
- Instagram: @possandruby
- Hear the full interview with Danielle on my podcast, *The Emma Lovell Show.*

10

BLEISURE HACKS

Can you travel the world and work at the same time? Yes. End of the chapter. Ha ha.

But seriously, you can—IF you plan for it.

In 2018, Mathew and I traveled for 49 days to eight countries around the world. I worked every week, but not every day. At the time, I was running my communications business and doing some work for the charity challenge and travel company Soulful Concepts. I wrote articles, made calls and followed up clients.

Before we left, I explained to Mathew that I needed to work on the trip. I had to bring in income and didn't want to shut down my business for seven weeks.

He was on leave from Sea World Australia and received his salary the whole time. This was a great comfort—for him. He agreed to me working during the trip because I planned it all and was clear about it. We agreed I would need three to four hours most days to work in peace. And not every day. He would sleep, explore or do whatever he felt like so I could focus.

I worked in:

- U.S.A.: Los Angeles, Chicago, Las Vegas and Boston.
- Mexico: Mexico City.
- U.K.: Surrey.
- Italy: Tuscany and Rome.
- Iceland: Reykjavik.
- Ireland: Wicklow, Galway and Dublin.
- Italy: Florence and Rome.
- Hong Kong.

I did not work in:

- Cuba: There is NO internet except in public parks—random—and I really enjoyed that pre-planned switch off for five days.
- Italy: Positano and the Vatican.

The secret of success is to plan. For example, I didn't think of it as a seven-week vacation. I thought of it as a trip where we celebrated with friends at their wedding in the U.S.A. and then later in the U.K. with my darling cousin at her wedding. We created amazing memories as a couple. And I didn't have to feel stressed about money.

Doing my work gave us both some space and solitude instead of being together for such a big chunk of time. This worked for us, and we've got better at it as the years go on.

AN INSPIRED QUESTION

The chapter is inspired by and takes some excerpts from an article I wrote for the magazine She Defined after that trip. As I mentioned in Chapter 7, it was called, "How I run my business and travel the world."

This whole book, and my business as a Bleisure coach, stemmed from a question my fab business colleague Kate Toon asked me one day: "How *do* you manage to travel quite so much and run a business?"

When I looked at that article, I realized that I combine business and travel in a unique way, and not everyone knows how to make it work. The idea for my new business offer as a Bleisure coach was born.

So, thank you Sharon Green, editor at She Defined. And thank you Kate Toon. You really did set me on the path for the Bleisure life.

BEFORE YOU LEAVE, PLAN

To work from anywhere, you must be incredibly organized. A structure and a plan ensure you meet your deadlines and have a great time. My calendar is my best friend. If it is not in my calendar, it won't happen. I also use time sheets, task lists and notes to prioritize my work.

Looking ahead at my travel itinerary and carving out periods for work also helps me to enjoy my leisure time while traveling. I allocate blocks of work and I am disciplined about it. Block out at least three to four hours each day you work so you get through a substantial amount. Then you have the morning or the afternoon or evening free to explore the new destination you're in.

These solid blocks of "work time" settle you into work mode. I have learned this from trying to fit in an hour here or there between sightseeing or transiting on various modes of transport, which is much more difficult for me.

If you're traveling with a partner or friend, be clear that you will be unavailable for these blocks of work hours but will spend time with them afterward.

Hopefully, you will avoid situations like my recent family trip to Mostar, Bosnia. I arrived to discover I had no global roaming on my phone, only Wi-Fi. I was knackered and didn't check my calendar before bed. We had changed time zones and I realized in the morning when checking my emails that I had missed a podcast interview with the amazing online course builder Tina Tower, for her case study for this book. She is only available every few months for interviews. Kindly, she explained we'd have to reschedule and six months later, we got it done. She was very understanding, but as a Bleisure artist herself, she mentioned that perhaps we could have rescheduled when I realized I'd be in Bosnia, with an unforgiving time zone. Noted, lovely Tina. Planning lesson learned.

Consider the following five aspects of your Bleisure trip to plan it so you never repeat that silly mistake. Instead, you have a wonderful, productive and organized time. Whether you are working with a full-time job or for yourself, the planning is much the same.

1. Know your numbers.
2. Be upfront with clients.
3. Be upfront with loved ones.
4. Know your time zones.
5. Identify Wi-Fi black spots.

1. Know your numbers

Create a budget. You will reduce so much stress. To get started, ask yourself:

- What are your normal living expenses, weekly or monthly?
- What, if any, expenses will you have to meet while away?
- What are your travel expenses going to be?
- What are the opportunity costs of your trip? Will you miss business events or work opportunities, for example?
- How much buffer have you got if things don't go to plan? (Do as I say not as I did not do. Though I'm getting much better with building the buffer now.)
- How many hours of work can you do per day? At your destination? En route? (These days make it harder.)
- How much will you earn while you are away?
- What income, if any, might you win as you travel or because of your travels?
- How much do you want this trip?

I love planning out a trip and budgeting the cost ahead. I use my beloved spreadsheet-database, Airtable, to map it all-out, plan destinations and my spending. I include flights, trains, car hire, buses, accommodation, activities, spending and a buffer. I'm pretty darn good at it these days. I usually land within a couple of hundred dollars of my planned spend because I sit down and do the numbers first.

You can find my trip planning resource at the website: emmalovell.au/bleisurebook.

2. Be upfront with clients or employers

I am very clear with my clients: just because I'm sitting near a beautiful beach in Mexico or cycling around the temples of Cambodia doesn't mean I'm not ready to work. I have my laptop and phone and that's my office. Tell people where you will be and what times you'll be available. They will have clear expectations and won't make assumptions. Set achievable deadlines with colleagues or clients that take your schedule into account, then knuckle down and do the work.

Be honest about when you will get your work done. In the past, I've been so unrealistic about what I can achieve and have made meetings at silly times. If someone asks if you're available at a certain time and you aren't sure, just say you're not available. It saves a lot of stress and disappointment on both sides and meets everyone's expectations.

When you talk about work with an employer or client you say, "Hey, I'm going to be working from Hawaii next month. I will be perfectly productive. But after our meeting, I'm going to jump in the pool." Most people will be impressed by this dedication, commitment, efficiency and honest communication. And if they're not that's on them.

3. Be upfront with loved ones

"But you're on vacation. Why are you doing work?" As I mentioned earlier, this is often the response I get when I tell people I work while on "vacation." But remember, it's not a vacation for me. It is Bleisure: working while traveling. From time to time, I do take pure vacations and switch off. That is important. We'll cover this more in Chapter 11.

Many people can't fathom working while traveling. Travel equals vacation. But I explain that my working arrangements are the reason I travel so frequently.

When traveling with my partner, I always have a discussion with him before we go. I explain how I plan to fit work into our vacation schedule. He's then aware of the work I have to complete and the time I'll need to do it. Generally, I ask for a few hours a day of quiet time (and that could be at 10 p.m., if I choose). He can use this time to have a nap, go to the bar or do his own internet time while I work. Often, it doesn't impact our time together or hinder the amazing things we see and do. I do this to make sure we both have the same expectations of how we will spend our time.

Now with our son, Finn, along for the ride, we make arrangements to each get alone time. It can feel a bit like shift work, but while he's young, it is important. Mathew takes the time to sleep or go to the gym. I work or get on top of my schedule and plans.

It doesn't always work out and that's OK. As I write this chapter at our Indian safari camp, I'm re-negotiating an extra 15 minutes to finalize these words. My husband argues with my son about an apple, while threatening to put him outside with the monkeys.

Everything I offer in this book is with the best intentions, but it doesn't always work out perfectly. Follow these steps and address these areas and you will have a much smoother time.

(We did not leave my three-year-old outside with the monkeys. He is healthy and well, if not just a little cheeky like the aforementioned monkeys.)

4. Know your time zones

The clock app on my phone is a lifesaver. Before I leave, I add my client's location and my home time zone. Wherever I'm going, I add the new time zone into the app. My laptop time is set to Brisbane, Australia, time. Most of my clients are in that time zone. Then I put my mobile and watch on local time, which helps when making appointments. I can easily compare the time zones.

Remember, just because it's 1 a.m. your time, doesn't mean you can't work. My clients used to gasp in horror when they found out what time I was working. But when you're traveling, you can choose your hours. I'm quite happy to work until 2 a.m. and then sleep until 10 a.m.

This changes with children; I don't have quite the same stamina to do that all the time when we travel as a family. But hey, with jet lag, sometimes I'm up at that time with him anyways, so may as well work while he watches a little TV before heading back to snooze land.

5. Identify Wi-Fi black spots

Without a good internet connection, there is no way I could work the way I do. Obviously, you cannot guarantee a good internet connection. So, when you do have a good connection, do the bulk of your work.

I make the most of programs such as Dropbox and Google Drive to upload photos and large files when the internet is reliable. I'll then do writing tasks when I know I'll be in remote areas where the internet may not be available, such as on long train or plane journeys. Offline mode for Google Docs is a game changer. That helped me write this book on planes, in safari camps and anywhere I could get out my laptop.

Spend extra on a good phone plan; you'll save later. So often I've had to use my personal hot spot or switch on roaming to get something to a client on time. Paying a little more for my phone plan means continuing to travel the world while I work. That's a choice I'm willing to make.

PLUS ONE

These five tips apply to the client-based work I do. But now, I have found a way to combine the business, travel and self-care and that is:

Retreats.

But more on that in Chapter 12.

Questions for reflection

Some questions for you to think about as you prepare to add more work into your travel or vice versa.

1. Does your work or business allow for flexible working?

2. Have you done your numbers for the trip?

3. Have you downloaded my trip planner? See emmalovell.au/bleisurebook.

4. Do you have global roaming, a phone dongle? Or are you willing to get them?

5. Could you Airbnb or let your place to travel a bit longer?

6. Can you start to communicate to your workplace or clients about being location independent and working from anywhere?

7. If you're not able to work from anywhere, what other income could you generate that you could work on while on vacation? E.g., buying more shares or doing some travel writing or doing some work in the tourism industry to enjoy some travel/vacation and subsidize the trip?

8. What other things would you need to set up in your business and work life to allow you more freedom to take longer breaks, travel more or work from anywhere?

Write them all down. This becomes your action plan.

Short and sweet

- Yes, you can: it's possible to travel and work at the same time if you plan.

- Budget: plan expenses and budget carefully.

- Make a work schedule: allocate dedicated work hours daily.

- Be honest with your clients or workplace: set expectations with clients, partners and travel companions.

- Have open communication with loved ones

- Know your time zones: understand and plan around time zones for smooth scheduling.

- Good internet: ensure reliable internet for the times you need to work.

- Flexible setup: prepare your home and work for operating remotely.

BEN SOUTHALL
Best job in the world

Sometimes the people you meet just stick in your mind. Ben Southall is one of those people. Ben Southall is an adventurer and entrepreneur, best known for winning the "Best Job in the World" competition hosted by Tourism Queensland in 2009. The job? Living on Hamilton Island in the Great Barrier Reef and promoting it to the world. Since then, Ben has written a book called *The Best Job in the World: How to Make a Living from Following Your Dreams*. He founded Best Life Adventures, a company that takes people on unique and challenging travel experiences.

Ben and I met in the most random way, when my husband went to look at a motorbike he might buy off him, but our life paths had so much in common. It was meeting Ben that sparked my husband and I to find our dream location for our eventual dream home, which is the region where Ben lives. His approach to life inspires me. He continues to travel with his wife and young son. He has been a guiding light for me pursuing a life I love and doing differently.

Ben jumped at the chance to reconnect—as is his life pattern—and to be in this book. I could not have written a book on Bleisure without his philosophy and approach in it.

Can you start by describing your business?

My job now is running a business taking people on adventures. We have our base market, which is our corporate stuff, giving companies and businesses an opportunity to do things outside of a boardroom. We strip them of their phones and take them to places like Moreton Island [Queensland] or Tasmania for retreats.

How long have you been working this way?

After winning the "Best Job in the World" in 2009, I leveraged that experience to build my career. I founded Best Life Adventures. This whole snowball was a six-month journey to get to the final of the best job in the world, and that was nearly 16 years ago now.

Winning the competition brought worldwide attention and opened many doors for me. It was life changing. I had already documented my travels in Africa, so transitioning to a career where I could continue sharing my adventures and inspiring others felt natural.

Why did you start?

I lost two people in my life at a young age. Friends my age. It kickstarted something internally that said you've got one chance. This is it. Get out there and do it, otherwise, you'd be stuck here (living in the U.K.).

You love to travel and try to do it as much as you can. Why is that?

Travel became my best place for learning about me and about the world. I studied and did my degree, but it wasn't my happy place. Travel opened up at the right age—at 21—where you're still learning and growing as a human.

How have you included travel in your work?

I set up the travel company Best Life Adventures because I need to get people outside of Australia to experience those mad places in the world that I've been to.

Did you always set out to travel and work?

My first summer job out of university was to go out to Cape Town and work on the ground there for three months doing the around-the-world yacht race. That gave me the taste for it.

What's your advice for someone looking to include more travel in their life?

There's always a reason not to go. Accountability is a huge part of doing it. So go out there and say, "I'm off to do this. This is my date."

Do you think the Bleisure life is possible and sustainable?

Yeah, it's hard work because sometimes you never have the "off time." My life has become my business and my business has become my life. But if you love what you do enough, you never work a day in your life.

What do you enjoy about traveling with your kid?

Sharing it all with him. We're taking [my son] Atlas to Botswana next year. I'll be there for two and a half weeks in self-driving four-wheel-drives as I did around Africa. We'll be staying in camps where any animal can just walk up to the tent at night.

What's your dream destination to work in?

One place that comes to mind is the Magadi Gadi salt pans in Botswana. There are Baobab trees there. It is not influenced by anything on the planet. It's a place to go write a book. It's a place to just be. It's a real Zen place.

CONNECT WITH BEN

- Website: bestlifeadventures.com
- Instagram: @bestlifeadventures
- Hear the full interview with Ben on my podcast, *The Emma Lovell Show.*

SWITCH OFF

Jobs fill your pocket. Adventures fill your soul.
– Jamie Lyn Beatty

IT'S OK TO HAVE A VACATION

You might think as you read this book, "Do I always have to take my family on my work trips? Am I meant to make money from every travel experience?" Don't worry. I've had these concerns. And sometimes I cram too much into a single trip.

Most people love vacations, including me. Sometimes we all need to switch off and do very little. I advocate for pure leisure and the combo of business and leisure. Whether it's a quick getaway or an intrepid adventure, making time for you and stepping out from day-to-day life gives you a new perspective on work and life. It's totally OK to just have a vacation. Really.

Bleisure works for me when I allocate time to work and time to switch off. At times I've taken the Bleisure concept too far. I'd take my work away with me and try to meet deadlines when I just needed a break. Sometimes even a Bleisure coach needs to rest and just be.

The Rose Farm Retreat

Money mindset mentor Denise Duffield-Thomas holds retreats at her amazing property, the Rose Farm. I went to one in August 2023. I was so excited to see the property I'd heard so much about from Denise. As I run retreats, I thought going to the retreat would have a dual function: it would be great for me to manifest success, and I planned to share the entire experience with my audience and market my upcoming retreats.

But in Denise's welcome, she talked about making the retreat a sacred space, and enjoying the experience of giving ourselves time and space. Soon after the welcome talk, I picked up some cards created by Rebecca Campbell, which she calls The Rose Oracle. You draw a card and read the mystical teachings on them. I pulled the card "sub rosa." Rebecca says in Roman times, sub rosa referred to having private conversations under the roses. As a card, it means there are secrets, ideas and feelings you keep just for yourself.

This retreat was for me as a participant. Often, I'm the retreat host and working. But this time, the retreat was an investment in me, and I didn't have to share it. During that retreat, I also realized that I don't have to monetize everything. Some things can just be. I captured photos and took lessons for myself. Even now, there's so much of that retreat I haven't shared with others. It's OK to have things just for you too, in case you also need that permission. You're allowed to switch off from the social media and sharing cycle too.

Retreat + family trip + running the business

I love proving that the Bleisure life can work. But one trip to Melbourne was so hectic, I realized I needed to slow down. I had a 6 a.m. flight from the Gold Coast to Melbourne, which meant I was up at 4 a.m. That put me on the back foot from the start.

I met my business collaborator Jade Warne in the airport. We started talking business and ideas straight away. We met a client for a coffee, then caught up with another colleague, self-worth advocate

Farah Mak, and captured content for social media. That afternoon we hosted a private photoshoot before drinks with two clients.

The following day, I hosted a 9-5 retreat day. I organized three private photoshoots for people attending the retreat too that were strategically spread throughout the day. This was an amazing way to make the best use of the space I had hired and increase our income from the one event, but meant I was "on" all day, with no rest breaks. I'd also planned networking drinks that evening so my clients and colleagues could connect. Eighteen people turned up. Amazing. I went to dinner with two colleagues from the drinks before Mathew and Finn arrived at 9 p.m. Mathew had worked all day, and Finn had fallen asleep and re-awoken. We were all exhausted. The next morning, Finn woke at 5 a.m. Ouch. At that moment, I regretted my life choices for a little while.

Are you tired reading all that? Cos I sure am. That was in the space of just two days.

Mathew, Finn and I then had a few chill days. But it took me a while to let go of the idea that we needed to be making more of our time away. I thought relaxing was a waste of time instead of recognizing that we all needed the slower pace.

Lesson? It's OK to have a business trip and add in a bit of social. And I don't have to bring my family on every work trip, every time. Also, I can go to hotels with my boys and have a pleasant stay and not have to work while there. Or I can go to reccy the hotel ahead of an event, if I really want to monetize it. (Hey, it's still me we're talking about.)

Tiger tour, hosting a journo and family vacation

OK, we are seeing a pattern here—I try to squeeze a lot in. I think you've seen the extreme side of me by now. I had an idea to visit India in June 2024. Originally, it was for a party with colleagues and to see the Indian tigers with my boys.

So why not make it into a tour and invite others along? Also, while we're at it, let's promote my affiliate partner, the luxury travel company

Indus Bound, to a wider audience. Invite a skilled travel writer to come along and pitch stories about it. Cue travel writer Lindy Alexander. As we made the itinerary, I chatted with Lindy about hosting a journalist through Indus Bound and the stories she'd want to see. Then we arranged our dates as a family.

Then a friend in Delhi, Neha Gupta from Saffron Palate, asked me a simple question: "Why did I never have a vacation in Delhi?" I've met Neha several times when I've taken clients to her fabulous cooking classes. She said it was lovely to see me so often, but I was always in Delhi for a short time and always hosting clients.

I explained the trip was for work, and I'd spent lots of time on vacation in Delhi in the past. But then her words sank in. I love Delhi. I love India. But I'm always working there now. I'm not taking time to soak in the country I love and enjoy it like I used to.

I scrapped the tour and put the hosting plans on hold. There's plenty of time for that. I can make the work trip a dedicated trip. That trip became a vacation again. We saw five tigers on two safaris, magical moments I enjoyed with my darling boys. What a gift. During those safaris and at the beautiful wilderness camp, I switched off completely so I could just be.

WHAT DOES YOUR VACATION LOOK LIKE?

The Oxford Dictionary defines a vacation as: "a period of time spent traveling or relaxing away from home." But I'd argue that vacations at home are also refreshing, especially if you travel a lot for work. Exploring your own backyard can be as exciting and invigorating as an overseas getaway.

Vacations look different for everyone. For some, it's doing nothing. For Mathew, time at home is pure joy. For others, it's about something physical and adventurous, like a trek in New Zealand or a cycle tour in Cambodia. Or perhaps it's lying on a beach at an all-inclusive resort and being taken care of. But you get to decide. It's whatever your body and mind are calling for. It's whatever switching off looks like to you.

I can meditate. I once did a 10-day silent Vipassana meditation retreat. But meditating isn't always easy for me, so I go on a one-day or three-day refresher from time to time. Sometimes, my meditation looks like a walk in nature, getting into a groove, getting out of my head and into the wilderness.

I love cruises to the surprise of some friends. I often hear people saying, "Cruises are not for me." But hey, have you tried it? What I love about cruises is they allow me to switch off because my accommodation, food and entertainment are all in one place and I don't have to think. I can do lots or nothing. And now I have a family, cruises are even better because I don't have to think for them either. And did I mention they have a kids club?

Different ways to travel will appeal at different stages of your life.

Switched off travel options

Here are some ways I've traveled and switched off over the years:

- Cruises.
- Packaged tours.
- Luxury tours: Indus Bound.
- Travel with a charity or a social goal.
- Solo travel in any of these ways.
- Retreats: Writing. Health. Yoga. Silent, such as Vipassana.
- Bleisure: taking rest time at the destination after a work event.
- Weekends away.
- One night away.
- Stay at a friend's house.
- Staycation: stay home and kick everyone else out.

You don't have to do Bleisure on every trip. Set aside vacations just for fun, relaxation or rejuvenation. Let's reflect on this chapter and work out what switching off means to you.

"Different ways to travel will appeal at different stages of your life."

Questions for reflection

Write your answers to add to your Bleisure life action plan.

1. What does a vacation mean to you?

2. Where do you want to go on vacation next?

3. What do you like doing on vacation?

4. How do you relax?

5. Who do you like to travel with?

6. Would you consider a solo vacation?

7. Have you ever done a package or organized tour vacation?

8. Would cruises be an option for you?

9. Can you make some time to switch off and vacation at home?

10. How can you take time for you, even when you can't travel far? (More about this in Chapter 15.)

Short and sweet

- Switching off is OK.

- Define your boundaries for Bleisure. You don't always have to add work to a trip.

- You can do things just for you; it doesn't always have to be monetized.

- Don't overload your trips with business and leisure and family.

- Diversify your travel style. Different stages of life may call for different trips.

- Staying at home for a vacation can be as refreshing as traveling.

- Find what works for you.

12

RETREATS: THE ULTIMATE BUSINESS, TRAVEL AND SELF-CARE

The sun kissed the water and shone into my face. The light momentarily distracted me from my laptop and I looked around. We drifted along in our two-bedroom houseboat through the backwaters of Kerala, Southwest India. I sat up the front, cross-legged and staring out at the palm trees lining the banks.

That was January 2019. I was hosting a tour through India for 16 days with my travel partner (then called Take me to India, now Indus Bound). I saw it as an opportunity to test my idea, which was to host trips for women who wanted to travel through India but had no one to go with. Either they were single, or their partners and friends did not want to go. I wanted to show women the beautiful India I know and love.

Then I had a thought. *What if I bought a group of women back here and ran a retreat in the capital of Kerala, at the five-star hotel the Fragrant Nature Cochin and then on the houseboat?*

Five and a half years later, I sat on that same houseboat with a group of five people, plus a photographer, two of their partners and two children. We had just come here from the Fragrant Nature Cochin hotel. I realized—I've done it. I manifested this retreat dream into reality.

That was my first international business retreat, and there was nowhere else I would have held it but India. It's a truly remarkable experience to realize that you are living a life you designed for yourself. To set a goal in one spot, and return to it and say, "I did it." That's the power of travel and, of course, goal setting and manifestation.

WHY I LOVE RUNNING RETREATS

Retreats are the ultimate combo of travel, business and self-care.

By now, you have many ideas about how to travel the world, make money and live a life you love now. I've shared almost all I know with you. But I've never experienced such a beautiful marriage of my passions and interests as I have with hosting retreats. It's the pinnacle of Bleisure.

I am often asked, "Emma, what is your primary business" or "Emma, what do you do?" Well, let's be honest: that's a question I've been asked my entire career. And I think I will always be asked how I make my living because seeing someone travel the world, do what they love and get paid for it is rare. And it's rarely celebrated. ("Hello, tall poppy," as we Aussies say.)

In the last few years, retreats and training others in how to run them has become a big focus. I love running retreats because they are such a tangible offer and are much easier to explain than my personal branding work.

When I am hosting a retreat, it's my job to hang out with amazing people in beautiful locations and get well paid to do it. And I do not mean just covering my expenses. I mean making a profit from every retreat I run. This is my lane. This is where I shine.

And these days I do more than host retreats. Now I teach others how to host retreats, and to do it profitably as I do.

I've seen how they've transformed people's lives and opened them up to so many opportunities.

Look, running retreats may not be for you, but before you decide, I want to share HOW they work and WHY they are such a big part of my business today, and will be an even bigger part of my future … another book in the making … watch this space.

WHAT IS A RETREAT?

A retreat is when you go away with a group of people to a luscious, beautiful, amazing place, and offer them some sort of transformation. Retreats can be about anything, provided there is a transformation attached to the experience. Typically, people see retreats as health and wellness. But they don't have to be. You can go on retreats for writing, creativity, cooking, eating (food tours), extreme fitness, recuperation from an illness, a getaway from your family care duties (respite), and more.

In February 2024, my client Christine Kankkunen and I co-hosted a retreat called She Freights. Christine runs a logistics company, called Pivot Freight. The women on the retreat wanted to source products from India. So, she delivered information about freight forwarding and logistics as a retreat. I love that.

My meditation and yoga clients have the most success with retreats, as they really do go hand in hand. And when you take it one step further and add in India, home of yoga, as the retreat destination, it's a no-brainer.

WHY INDIA?

I've talked a lot about India in this book and have shared a few of the reasons I have such a strong connection with her. But chatting to a friend today and typing this chapter as I fly at 32,000 feet over the incredible land of India, I am reminded why it is such a powerful place for me and such a perfect destination for retreats.

I give a lot. I do a lot. I know that. And I'm a nurturer at heart. And, throughout this book process and throughout my journey, I've also needed nurturing. It dawned on me as I spoke to my friend that I love India so much because I feel nurtured and embraced by India. India is a land of service. Going there now, I will be served. I will be cared for and nurtured back to my full heart. It inspires me beyond belief and forces me to really be present and connect with LIFE. My money mentor Denise Duffield-Thomas says, "I serve so I deserve." And I do serve. A lot. I know this book will serve you, for example.

In India's diverse, dynamic and contrasting culture, you see life's stark realities, unmistakable and inescapable. Life and death. Nature and development. Old and new. India impacts you.

You don't see India. You don't smell it, taste it, touch it or hear it. You feel it. India gets under your skin and enlivens the senses like no place I've ever known. India is hands down my favorite country in the world. Some of my most transformative experiences have happened here. It is part of me and I would love the opportunity to share it with you, even if it is just by you reading about it here.

REST AND RECEIVE

If you choose to step into the world of retreats as an attendee or a host, I know the magic awaits you, too. When you put your desires, your goals and your vision out into the universe, the universe will do all in its power to bring them to fruition. But you must get clear on what you want. That's what India gives me. Clarity. And that's what I deliver to clients on my "Rest & Receive" retreats.

We rest. We get clear. We ask for what we want and then … we can receive. I've met people from every walk of life and all levels of society. Hosting retreats and tours in India gives me the chance to give back to India by bringing people to this incredible land to experience it for themselves. I invite you to be open to India. Learn about her complexities, her strengths, her challenges and her uniqueness.

I want to create a space where my gorgeous clients, network and other amazing leaders can come together because India is like a second homeland to me. I am so delighted to be returning there right now, and writing this section of the book on the plane as we fly above it.

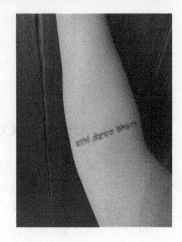

Athiti Devo Bhava is the unofficial motto of India. It means "guest is god." The kindness, generosity and hospitality I have experienced in India on my 15 visits here over the past 19 years are so profound that I now have that motto tattooed on my arm.

RETREATS AND SELF-CARE

As I wrote in Chapter 4, self-care can be a challenge. For me, going to bed on time every night can be a battle. But ask me if I want to go to India—or, one better, run a retreat there—and I'll move heaven and earth to make it happen.

Retreats are self-care.

India is my self-care.

Travel is my self-care.

Running a business that I love is my self-care.

And you can experience Bleisure through the magic of retreats. I hope you have felt inspired by this chapter to offer retreats, no matter what your work situation. So, if you are thinking about running one, even if you're just a little curious, I have some tips below. I also have done some wonderful podcasts on this topic on *The Emma Lovell Show*.

TOP TIP: GO ON A RETREAT BEFORE YOU HOST ONE

Go on a retreat before running one, always. You will learn what they are and how to run one. You will find growth and transformation in the short, dedicated period of a retreat that is nothing short of life-changing. Any time you can create a retreat, anywhere in the world, is such a gift. And you will get a better understanding of what people are looking for in your retreats.

HOW TO RUN A PROFITABLE RETREAT

I have learned a lot of lessons along the way about what to do and what not to do. But the biggest no-no I kept hearing was people saying they would run retreats on a break-even basis or even at a loss.

This is not a great way to go into a business activity. Don't start with, "I'll probably make a loss." From doing this myself, I know running at a loss or break-even leads to burnout and resentment. By the time you get on the retreat, you are over it. And you don't want to run one again.

I believe there are five guidelines to follow for running profitable retreats time after time. Avoid the pitfalls and focus on what's important and you'll enjoy profitable retreats that allow you to do what you love and change the lives of others.

1. Set a clear intention

Ensure your retreat has a clear purpose that speaks directly to a problem your dream audience wants to solve. Get clear on your WHY and this will be your guiding light for your retreat experience.

2. Price for profit

The biggest mistake I see with retreats is people not putting an appropriate margin on top of the costs of a retreat. Work out the expenses of running your retreat, then I recommend at least doubling it to factor in payment for you as the host, meeting your tax requirements, a 10%-15% profit margin and a buffer. So the price of your retreat now includes not just expenses, but also takes care of you and has accounted for a margin of error.

You do not need to run your retreat in India, but for my money, it is one of the easiest and most effortless destinations and your dollar goes so much further. You can experience seven-star service and luxury that is simply unattainable for the same price in other destinations.

3. Program with space

Make sure your retreat program isn't just a schedule—it should be a journey of transformation for your participants. Think about the logistics, the inclusions and avoid the overwhelm of over-delivery. But most importantly allow plenty of time for rest and spaciousness in your itinerary, this is where the magic happens.

4. Market, market and market

Don't keep your retreat a secret. Your marketing strategy must ensure your audience hears about your event in enough places and enough ways that they can't say, "Oh, I didn't know you run retreats." Share, share, share. Don't stop talking about it. If you think you've talked about it too much, you're probably getting to the right level of market-ing. Also, create a waitlist before and after your retreat. It's a powerful form of social proof and makes filling the spots a heck of a lot easier.

5. Customer care is paramount

Retreat-goers want the red-carpet treatment. Retreats are luxury ser-vices that clients choose to nurture and care for themselves. Deliver this care from the moment a client enquires about the experience until long after it is over. If you do this, they will become your raving fans and your best brand advocates.

Questions for reflection

1. What is a retreat?
2. Have you been on a retreat? What did you like or not like?
3. Do you want to run retreats? (If not, maybe move on now ha ha.)
4. Why do you want to host a retreat?
5. What's stopped you from hosting retreats in the past?
6. What do you feel is the most challenging part about hosting a retreat?
7. If you could host a retreat anywhere in the world, where would it be?
8. When would you run it?
9. Who is it for?
10. How many people will you have?
11. What will you include?
12. Who will help you?
13. How does it fit in with your current work?
14. How will you promote it?
15. How could you make running retreats a priority?

Great. Now you know if you want to run a retreat or not. If you're keen on running one, going through these questions and writing out the answers will give you a great blueprint to get started. And if you get stuck, call me. I know someone who's pretty good at teaching about this stuff. (Wink.)

Short and sweet

- Retreats combine travel, business and self-care, making money while enjoying beautiful locations. Bleisure at its best.

- Retreats can cater to different audiences and industries and focus on many themes including business, creativity, wellness and many more.

- Successful retreats require clear intentions, balanced programming, profitable pricing, effective marketing and excellent customer care.

- India offers a nurturing and inspiring environment, making it an ideal retreat destination.

- I am hosting more retreats around the world and teaching others to run successful retreats. Have I inspired you too?

TINA TOWER
The life and business of your dreams

You have one life.

Tina Tower believes this so strongly that it's the theme of her first book: *One Life: How to Have the Life of Your Dreams.*

Tina Tower is a dynamic entrepreneur who started her journey at 20, founding a tutoring center that evolved into a franchise, Begin Bright. This grew to 35 centers and 120 staff before Tina sold the business in 2016.

Tina then began business coaching, creating a successful online course while traveling the world for a year with her family, visiting 28 countries. Tina's empire now focuses on helping others package their expertise into online courses through Her Empire Builder. Her goal is to assist 100 women to each create businesses turning over $1 million a year by 2025.

Tina is the author of two bestsellers and a winner of prestigious awards. She advocates for "profit for purpose." For example, she supports education for young women in Kenya. She operates her digital empire from her farm on the Australian east coast.

Tina is a generous, passionate and excited human who wants to see other women in business succeed. I love having her as a cheerleader and she really knows how to motivate, inspire and encourage.

Tina was a must for a case study in this book because she manages to combine business and travel in the most fun and exciting ways. Raising the bar for herself and all of us, each time.

Can you start by describing your job or business?

I'm an entrepreneur. My current business that I have, which I think is probably going to be my longest lasting, is Her Empire Builder.

How long have you been working this way?

I started my entrepreneurial journey with a primary tutoring center and an educational toy store when I was 20. Over the years, I have adapted and evolved my business model. Currently, I focus on online education and coaching through Her Empire Builder.

How did you come to integrate travel into your business?

There's nothing I love more than combining business and travel. My husband and I, right from the moment we met, have been on at least two overseas trips every year—even when we were broke. Travel has always been a priority for us, and we've taken our kids on month-long trips every year since they were born.

Can you share an example of how you combine work and travel?

I've done destination launches for my courses from places like Hawaii, Mexico, and various locations in the United States and Australia. It gives the launches a different energy and makes them more exciting.

How do you manage your work schedule when traveling? And how does self-care and travel fit in?

I take the third week of every month off and do not schedule work on Thursdays and Fridays. This flexibility allows me to travel frequently while still managing my business effectively. When I'm away and I'm working there's no fluff. There's no procrastinating … you open that computer, you do it, and you get back to eating your gelato.

What are some of the sacrifices you've made to achieve this lifestyle?

In the early days, we lived frugally to prioritize travel. We didn't go out to restaurants or buy unnecessary items. Now, the sacrifices are less, but we still make conscious choices. For example, we calculated our retirement needs and decided on a balance between investing for the future and spending on travel.

What advice would you give to someone looking to include more travel in their work or business?

Sometimes we forget that we can work from anywhere. Pick a place you love and go. Working while traveling teaches you a lot about productivity because you learn to focus and get things done quickly.

What's your dream destination to work in?

I have been to nearly all my dream destinations. Tenerife in Spain is still on my list. I'd like to go and spend a few months there working. Another place on my list is Antarctica, although that might be more for adventure than work.

CONNECT WITH TINA

- Website: tinatower.com
- Instagram: @herempirebuilder
- Hear the full interview with Tina on my podcast, *The Emma Lovell Show.*

13

TRAVELING WITH KIDS

"Would you like us to page a doctor?"

Finn has just vomited all over himself, the seat and me for the second time and my mind races.

Is this really happening? Tears well in my eyes. Overwhelm is setting in. *What am I doing here alone? Do I really want a doctor to be called for my 15-month-old at 32,000 feet in the air? How serious is this?*

"Yes, please," I say. It is mid-April 2022 and COVID-19 is still very much a thing. This is my first trip overseas with Finn. I am alone. Because of the time off work and the cost of us all going, I'd decided to take Finn to meet his great-great cousin, then 99-year-old Bill Hunter, in America and his great grannie in England without the help of my husband. My first international flight with Finn and we had an emergency.

Thankfully, a midwife is on board. She assures me he is fine and advises me not to force him to eat, and to give him small sips of water. The cabin manager assures me that vomiting on an international flight is very normal for young children and that it probably isn't anything more serious. Their ears don't equalize, and the pressure can cause nausea. He's been on 12 domestic flights before, but the planes fly much higher for international flights. He is also a bit congested, and we suspected he might have been getting conjunctivitis the day before. It was a combination of factors.

Our kind cabin crew member comes over and asks me if there is anything more I need. With the second vomit, I am now out of clothes. I was proud of packing a second set, but now I know—you need at least two extra sets. "I know they are only for business class passengers, but I am also out of clean clothes," I say. "Is there any chance you can bring me a pair of the Qantas pajamas?" These happen to be my favorites, and thanks to my own travels and my dad's frequent business class trips, I have many sets at home. But today, I need these. She brings them over with a kind smile and replaces my vomit-sodden blanket with a quilt from business class. I so appreciate the support.

A BLIP IN THE SCHEME OF THINGS

This chapter is for you if you have kids or might want to one day. So, surely an experience like this would scare even the most ambitious traveler off, right? No way. Not even a bit. Yes, it was a gross, scary and overwhelming first flight. This was still in the height of COVID-19, and Australia had only just re-opened its borders. I had been so focused on getting out of the country and whether I would be allowed to leave. I was afraid of testing positive to COVID-19 on or near departure day. I hadn't had time to worry about what the flight with little Finn might hold.

On top of this, we had another leg of the trip—a four-hour flight to Chicago. Fortunately, we both slept. But upon landing, he threw up again. My poor boy was so sick. After 27 hours of travel, we had made it to our destination. And it was worth it. To see his 99-year-old cousin's face light up and to hand Finn over for a hug. For Finn to know his family. Admittedly, at 10:30 p.m. when I woke to Finn's crying after just 90 minutes of sleep, which led to a hellish first night, perhaps I questioned my life choices. (Just kidding.)

No, I wouldn't take any of it back. I did the best I could. The experience of introducing my baby to his cousin and then going on to the U.K. to meet his 92-year-old great-grandmother was priceless. I'll cherish those moments for the rest of my days.

I'm not going to gaslight you, though. It can be challenging. Had you asked me three days into a recent trip to India to write this chapter again, I would have re-written it as:

Don't!

The end.

There will be tough days, and I'll always share and be honest about those, as I did on my social media pages. Here's one Facebook post from that first trip with Finn when I was feeling the struggle. I also shared many gorgeous moments from our trip and loved seeing family and friends, but solo parenting and the jet lag was rough.

THE OTHER SIDE OF TRAVELING WITH A BABY

I've definitely commented about this over the past week or so, but the full force of the epic journey hit us last night. Jet lag is definitely a big deal for little babies and it's taking its toll on me, too. Some naps for us both to catch up through the day and what seemed like normal bedtime, but then not able to settle till 2 a.m. It's so hard to know what to do and basically, there's nothing. Just ride it out and keep us both calm.

The morning light (well, 11:30 a.m. light) makes things feel better, as well as big hugs from family. It is hard though.

More challenging than I could have imagined, and the days of unsettledness add up. We're OK and having a lovely day with special people. Taking time just to be with family and resting where we can.

But it's a blip in the grand scheme of things.

And for anyone who has kids, "Is being at home easy all the time?" The answer is, "No."

Whether you're traveling or at home, kids have moods, phases and stages. Some days are hard; some days are easy. You have moments of joy and moments of challenge. So, if that's the case, why not at least be in a fabulous destination while they throw their tantrum? Hell, I'll throw one too. Make it fabulous.

EXPECT TO BE ANXIOUS

Yes, it was daunting and challenging. If you haven't done it, I can understand why you might be afraid to. But it's just one day of challenge for a lifetime of memories. It's worth it. I hear from people how scared they are of flying with kids, and that it deters them from taking a trip. Even Mathew got anxious before his first long-haul flight with our son. But his anxiety was worse than the reality.

As you know, for me, travel isn't just about a vacation. It's not just something I do for fun and to accumulate experiences. It's about connection, family, and doing what is most important, which is sharing time with the ones I love. And the ones I love are scattered across the globe, so off we jet.

Finn is now three and a half. He's been on more than 50 flights and visited 12 countries. He's also been to five of the seven states and territories in Australia. Travel is normal for him. This is—and always will be—the life he knows. And sharing it with him that's a life I love. My darling, my sunshine is a world traveler already. He's a little champ.

"Where going?" he asks in his sweet little voice. He wants to know where we are, where we're going next and what adventures await. He loves to point to the photos of beautiful locations around the world on our TV screen saver and ask, "Can I go there?"

And I always reply, "Yes, baby. We can take you there."

Sometimes he recognizes the locations and says, "I've been there." It warms my heart that he knows and remembers the places he has been and feels excited by that. Although my opening story may have frightened you off, I am here to share with you that running a business or having your career, and traveling with a family are not mutually exclusive.

I hear people say to one another: "Now you have kids, you'll have to ease up on the travel." And to me, they rattle off the life stages and add, "You're going to have to slow down at some point when Finn goes to school."

Really? Of course, telling me I can't do something only makes me want to do it more and prove anyone who doubts me wrong. How many role models of traveling with kids do we need to stop giving each other advice like this? People pack up their family in a camper and travel around Australia. There are countless examples, so why not me? And why not you? Why is it only for "them?"

I travel with my child. I want to show you it's possible, too. I don't want to perpetuate this stereotype or for you to feel limited by the joy that is children. Our plan is to make the most of the next few years before Finn starts school. At the time of writing, we have at least one-and-a-half years. That's a lot of time to travel.

And when the school season of life starts, there are at least 13 weeks of school holidays in the public school system. That's a lot of time to fit in holidays and travel over the years. I'm quite excited about that prospect. It will give our family some routine. We will all know when I'm working, and when we are on vacation and can all head off together. When I was at university, I traveled during the semester breaks and, as you know from Chapter 3: She has the travel bug, I packed a lot in then. So, challenge accepted. We will make the most of the 13 weeks of school vacation every year. How far can we go, and what experiences can we get in?

"But Emma, it's more expensive in school vacation time," I hear you say. But not every destination is more expensive and not all school vacations align. And we know when school vacations are every year. So book and plan a long way ahead. You will make the most of the deals and savings.

NO EXCUSES

Give me an objection, and I'll give you a way to overcome it. I want to see people making the most of their lives and traveling, enjoying their leisure as much as possible, no matter what life stage they're at.

And you can do this with kids. Kids make you see the world in a new way; they constantly live with the beginner's mind. Let them help you experience travel in a whole new way.

Yes, Finn is only three now. But I promise you, I'll be writing a book called *Traveling with Kids* in the years to come and making regular updates as we go through the stages and ages of his life. Watch this space.

My friend, Sally Branson, whose consulting firm helps clients facing a crisis, travels with her six-year-old and seven-year-old boys during school holidays. And works the whole time. Because her work is intensive for short periods, she aims for a family mini break every six to seven weeks. She times them to take advantage of public holidays or pupil-free days. Schools usually give dates for both with 12 months' notice, so you can plan well in advance. This makes children good travelers on the domestic scale. She picks various locations and varying levels of luxury. There's nothing like a good old-fashioned brick motel in a country town with a breakfast hatch, two gigantic beds and a kidney pool.

Sally uses travel hacks like loyalty programs to reward hotel rooms to keep the costs down. Sally also travels with her kids overseas. Because they're a bit older than Finn, she makes sure they know that mummy working on vacation is part of the magic that makes vacations happen.

Here are Sally's tips for setting clear boundaries and working while traveling with kids:

- Online meetings either early in the morning or after the kids are in bed.
- Work during the day when the kids have down time. Kids don't have the stamina we do for travel, even if they think they do. They need rest breaks during the day.
- Limit work to necessary to-dos for clients and check-ins with staff.
- Have an out-of-office message explaining when you're available and how your clients can reach you urgently.

- Find an amazing coffee shop or Wi-Fi spot to work. It's work, but in a new location. Our brains operate more creatively in unfamiliar spaces. If you've got to do client work, it may as well be somewhere picture-perfect.

SOMETIMES IT'S EASY

Not every flight will be a horror story. My opening example was a baptism of fire. The next international flight we took as a family, where I had my husband for support, my son slept 11 of the 13 hours (of course) and we both got about six or seven hours' sleep, too. We have learned to stop over. We add a night in Los Angeles to adjust before arriving in Chicago. This provides a blissful catch-up and a lovely reset, so I don't feel like the earth is spinning beneath my feet and my body might fall to the ground like a ton of bricks at any moment.

I want to point out that with all the travel I've done and these trips with my son, I never stopped running my business. We've taken breaks and holidays of course and had downtime, but my business has always continued. The point is, you can run a business, travel the world, have a gorgeous family AND live a life you love.

As you read in Chapter 9: Work hacks, I now have an executive assistant (EA) in Australia and two virtual assistants (VAs). That's a tremendous help in keeping the business running and reducing the work pressure helps when I am traveling with Finn. They keep me on top of demands. I can check in and focus only on the tasks I need to do. Also, I now take pressure off myself by batching my podcast—doing several episodes at once when home so I can take a break when I'm traveling.

I'm still learning. It's a newish thing for me to travel with a child and the demands change. Managing my business and travel with my now three-and-a-half-year-old son differs from when he was 15 months. Now Finn is much easier to communicate with. He follows directions, and occasionally he'll walk by himself, meaning I don't have to carry him. I love sharing these changes on my podcast, too.

I've learned to slow down and not to include so much. To be a bit more realistic about how much I can achieve when Finn is with me, or when both my boys come along.

MY TOP TIPS FOR TRAVEL WITH KIDS

Maximize the travel while they're little

Take advantage of the fact that a child under two flies for free and often stays free in hotels. And plan as much travel as possible before they start school to avoid school holiday crowds and increased travel and accommodation expenses.

Be over prepared for the plane

Take at least three sets of clothes for your child and two extra sets of clothes for yourself. Children get sick on flights, and make a lot of mess generally, you must be prepared to clean up and do a costume change or two.

Pack light but smart

Prams and car seats are bulky. Can you borrow or buy these items at your destination and sell or donate them when you leave?

Stay in family-friendly accommodations

Look for family-friendly hotels or Airbnbs that offer bassinets, high-chairs and separate sleeping areas. This can make an enormous difference to your comfort and convenience. Choose accommodation that has activities for children, like pools or kids clubs. This keeps kids entertained and allows you to have some downtime. Sites like booking.com identify family-friendly accommodation.

Build in extra downtime

Don't overload your itinerary. Plan one activity daily and allow for plenty of rest and relaxation. Having a flexible schedule helps every-one enjoy the trip more.

Travel with friends or family

Having extra adults to help with childcare makes all the difference. Traveling with friends or family allows you to share responsibilities and gives you some time to spend on your own and with your partner. That is better than handing your child or children back and forth between parents like ships in the night. You will also feel a sense of familiarity and support and make your trip more enjoyable and less stressful. It also saves money.

Consider cruises

Cruises are made for families. They are cost-effective and convenient. Your accommodation, food and entertainment, all in one place, and you only need to unpack once. This is so much easier than, say, a road trip. And, they have a kids club—win.

Plan breaks in your travel

If your trip involves long flights or multiple legs, consider breaking it up with overnight stays. This can help everyone adjust and reduce travel fatigue.

Ask for help

Don't be afraid to ask for help from flight attendants, hotel staff, or even strangers if you need it. Most people are happy to help parents traveling with young children.

Embrace the adventure

Traveling with kids is challenging but rewarding. Focus on the memories you're creating and the experiences you're sharing as a family, not the difficult moments. The lovely ones are what will stick in your memory.

Questions for reflection

1. What type of travel do you like doing with kids?

2. What mode of transport would suit your child's current age range: plane, boat, train, car or bus?

3. How long would be a good trip for your family at this stage? Seven days, 10 days, two months? (For us, three weeks max is the sweet spot right now.)

4. How are you going to budget for a trip that includes the whole family?

5. List five destinations you would like to visit with a kid.

6. Who can come and help you?

7. What friends would you want to share a holiday with?

8. Could you afford or consider getting help for your trip, such as a nanny, babysitter or kids club?

9. How will you make time for yourself?

10. What will you do if things go curvy and plans need to change? e.g., have an alternative vacation plan, have insurance, bring a friend/family member to support if your partner can't attend.

Short and sweet

- You can run a business, travel the world, have a gorgeous family AND live a life you love.

- When you travel with kids, you may have to adapt and slow down a little.

- There are many ways to travel, and it doesn't just have to be club med or packaged holidays.

- Even if it's awful one time, it won't be like that every time.

- It's worth it, no matter their age, for the beautiful memories you get to share with them.

- Kids make you see the world in a new way. They constantly live with the beginner's mind. Let them help you experience travel in a whole new way.

YEMI PENN
Be unreasonable with your dreams

Yemi is a self-defined "curious rebel" dedicated to challenging the status quo to create a more just, equitable, diverse and inclusive world. She does this with grace, compassion, humor and a bit of cheeky rebellion.

She is an engineer by profession, thought leader by mission and author of *Did You Get the Memo? Because I F**king Didn't*. She has spoken at TEDxOcala in Florida, and been interviewed by Jack Canfield, the co-author of bestselling book series *Chicken Soup for the Soul*.

Yemi invites us to collectively ignite our rebellious curiosity, starting with ourselves.

Yemi doesn't understand the word "can't." It would only challenge her curiosity and she will find a way that she can, if it serves her.

I met Yemi at the Business Chicks Movers + Breakers conference in 2022. We went deep, fast. That's the only way with Yemi. She is so open and curious that you can't help but be drawn into her orbit. I'm so grateful she created the time to share with you all. There's simply no one like her.

Can you start by describing your job or business?

My job is to be a curious rebel. And I laugh because it sounds so wank. But that's my job—to be a curious rebel in everything. A curious rebel as an engineer, a curious rebel as a speaker, as a writer, as a documentarian, as a researcher—all those things.

How long have you been working this way?

It was when I opened my gym, when I bought it. So, I'd say 2016. Eight years and it's only just started to ramp up. I changed the dial again to allow me to slow down. And then it's ramping up again.

How did you go from engineer to buying a gym?

Sounds random as hell. When I was at university in the United Kingdom, I remember wanting to be an aerobics instructor and I went through the YMCA. We used to call it "garage aerobics." There's this genre of music in the UK called "garage," which is all about reggae beats. The energy in the space was just divine. I remember feeling pure joy. Every Wednesday from seven to nine people knew not to bother me. When I had my daughter, there was always a friend in the neighborhood that could look after them. So, experiencing that kind of joy and community always made me want to be an aerobics instructor.

Do you love to travel? And why do you travel a lot?

I love to travel. I don't necessarily love the traveling experience to get there, i.e., the mode of travel. I'm one of those people that just wants to get there. But I love exploring the world. I want to say that with the caveat that every time I travel, I have made myself extremely uncomfortable. I love it. And it's so uncomfortable. However, the feeling I get from experiencing something different is worth the discomfort.

Did you always set out to travel and work?

No. No. Most of my mode of travel is by plane, and I was an air sick child. So, at some point I may have made the decision: if I can't get to this place by foot or by road then it's not going to happen. So, I categorically did not [set out to travel]. But my desire to experience something different was just so strong.

How have you managed to now include travel in your work?

I've done traveling with work by breaking a lot of rules. By being unreasonable once again with my desires. I've done it by breaking a

"Because I'm living the life that I didn't even know I could dream of."

lot of the rules that I either gave myself or the one I was given, motherhood. And that's a tough one. You know when we say it for the fun of it, "It takes a village [to raise a child]." But it's true. And I appreciate I don't have the village that maybe I was born into but I can create one I trust.

What would be your advice for someone who's looking to include more travel in their work?

I just go back to, "why?" But be radically honest with "why."

Do you think Bleisure, the combination of business and travel, is possible and sustainable?

It depends on frequency and how we find rest in between. Because that question itself feels like it's still subscribing to the notion that you're meant to go to work and then have a holiday. Like remember that's the model. That's the memo that most of us have been born into and signed up to. So, of course it's possible. It's just the reframing of it.

I just spent five weeks in the United States and people are asking me, "Was that for work or for pleasure?" And I just came up with "pleasure." Thanks for the combination though, Bleisure. That is literally what I wanted to say. It was for work but I made sure I found joy in that. Because I'm living the life that I didn't even know I could dream of. So absolutely.

Is it sustainable? It depends on what people define as sustainable. So that you're not burned out constantly? So, you can always have the same amount of money? Because that's the other sacrifice; there's times when I don't know when the income is coming in. And there's times when there's lots of income. The quality that I built from living a life where I do travel for work is equanimity, which is yummy. I find joy in the high but also find joy in the low.

How do you make time for self-care and to find some balance in your schedule?

I just don't f*ck about with my self-care. Like I just don't. It's a fine balance between trying to care for myself but also being an achiever. I do love achieving but I can't do it at the risk of my health. And as I get older my body and my hormones are doing different things that I have to adjust to. I listen to my body and it keeps the score by way of distressing events but also by way of wisdom. I know that if my eye is twitching, "Girl, you need to sleep." I know that if my shoulders all of a sudden feel like I've got 20 monkeys on it, it's because I'm carrying something emotionally based on a conversation I've had. I've got to figure out ways to really listen to my body because she's so damn amazing.

What's your dream destination to work in?

I don't think I've been there yet. I was going to say somewhere in Europe but I just had South America come and say, "Hey." It's weirdly in some Amazon forest type place that hopefully has Wi-Fi.

(To this I responded that I would be joining her; to let me know and I'll book the ticket. That's the kind of friend I am.)

CONNECT WITH YEMI

- Website: yemipenn.com
- Instagram: @yemi.penn
- Hear the full interview with Yemi on my podcast, *The Emma Lovell Show.*

14

THE TRAVELER MINDSET

TRAVEL AT HOME

"I don't want to be here. I want to go back overseas," my brother moaned to me, having just arrived home after two and a half years spent traveling. He surprised me. Two months before he left on his big trip, he'd told me with the same conviction, "I don't like traveling." But then, off he went, loved it, and never wanted it to end.

I knew how he felt coming back. I had a year away living it up when I was 18 and, when I came home, crashed back to reality. So, I felt I could impart some wisdom from my experience navigating the post-vacation or gap-year blues.

"See your city with fresh eyes, James. A lot has changed since the last time you lived here. You get the chance to see your home with your new world view. Just think of your home here the way you thought about London and Europe. There, you always looked for new things to do and different places to go. Keep that travel mindset now you're back."

Or something like that. This conversation was about 12 years ago. It was probably longer and a bit more rough and ready, but you get the gist. When you're not traveling, you can still have the traveler mindset and enjoy wherever you are.

THINK, FEEL AND ACT

Travel isn't just about visiting another location. It's about the way you think, feel and act when you get there. You feel energized, excited by the smallest thing. And then you get home and put your blinkers on. You don't allow yourself to see the wonders of what's right in front of you.

Often, when I'm overseas, I'm reminded of how special my home country is. I'm sitting somewhere in the world, explaining to a local, "Oh yes, we have kilometers of beaches just minutes from my home. Some of the world's best beaches are on my doorstep. You're right, I'm so fortunate to live in such a beautiful place."

Then it clicks. When was the last time I strolled along those beaches? Months ago. I haven't made the time to enjoy what's within my reach. I'm so grateful for those moments of realization. How fortunate I am and how accessible this beautiful life is. I'm thankful for those conversations that remind me, and I make a mental note to make more time as soon as I'm back.

AS IF FOR THE FIRST TIME

And I do. Sometimes it takes seeing our familiar surroundings in a new way to appreciate them. Children are so wonderful for helping us stay in this travel mindset. Or the "beginners' mindset," says Kerstin Pilz, my dear friend, writing mentor and author of Loving My Lying, Dying, Cheating Husband. That, she explains, is when you see and experience things as if for the very first time. You allow yourself to be caught up in the details and delighted by what is simple. The way the wind feels on your face, the colors of the sky at sunset, and the flavors as you bite into your lunch at a new cafe.

TRAVEL IN A MOMENT

You will find it easier if you put your phone down, take a breath and look around you. Be where you are. When you do this, you see and experience your home like a traveler. This book is about adding more of what you love into your life. Increase the amount of leisure and do more of what you enjoy. Live a life you love. Live it and embrace it—whether that's at home, abroad or anything in between.

You don't have to be on the go to travel. You can travel through your memories. You can travel in your mind and heart. You can travel with your attitude and approach to the world. You can have a bigger and wider world view. And you can simply apply the joys of travel to being at home.

Sometimes life takes away travel or leisure or what you love. Then you must use your traveler mindset to experience every day in a fresh way. It is crucial. For my brother and his wife, who met while they lived in London, life looks very different now. Louis, their gorgeous son, my darling nephew, very sadly passed away after just two and a half short years in this world. They devoted those years to his happiness. Extensive, and certainly international, travel was off the cards.

By applying the traveler mindset, my brother and his wife saw and did more than others have in their entire lives. They embraced local activities and tried new things to give their son Louis the best possible life.

LIVE YOUR LIST

We've all heard of a bucket list. It goes like this: "Oh goodness. I only have this amount of time left. I must tick off all these experiences." But a "life list" is different. I first heard of the life list when I read Kate Christie's book *The Life List: Master Every Moment and Live an Audacious Life*. She defines the life list as: "a list of everything she wanted to do and be while she was still young enough to enjoy it." Kate had experienced a series of life tragedies in five years that jolted her into action.

Now she pursues a life she loves. I shared this idea with my brother in those very early difficult weeks after Louis' diagnosis, and he created Louis' life list.

Just before Louis' passing, James said, "We are also unable to travel anymore, which sucks, but that's our life currently. Our vacations are Bear Cottage (a palliative care unit for children in Sydney) right now which has become an exciting time and something to look forward to.

"We are giving Louis his best life possible and obviously creating cherished memories, but we are also suffering with the inevitable known fate in the meantime."

The time to change is now. Adopt the traveler mindset. Create your life list. You don't have to wait until you can get on a bus, boat, train or plane. Don't let an awful tragedy be the catalyst for change. You can do that now. You can have goals, dreams and plans.

THE GRASS ISN'T ALWAYS GREENER

In 2022, I had decided that, as Finn grew, we needed more space. We live in an apartment on the Gold Coast. It's a great location and a super nice block, but we live on the third floor with a balcony. I wished we had a garden.

I was listening to Denise Duffield-Thomas' audiobook *Get Rich, Lucky Bitch*. She wanted to live in an area she could not afford. One way she upgraded her life was to rent in that area. I realized buying our dream home—or bigger home dream—was a few years away, but we could rent a bigger home. That could be our upgrade.

I suggested this to Mathew and he was on board. Running the numbers, it stacked up. We could afford a bit of an increase, still live in the same area, which we enjoyed, and move to a townhouse with a yard for Finn to play in.

We seriously indulged in this plan for six months. In February 2023, we even applied for a rental and got it but my husband had doubts. He wasn't ready. I would not do it unless we were both on board. The timing didn't work.

REST AND RECEIVE

In May 2023, I felt burned out and sick of the grind. I was stuck back in the feast-and-famine cycle and it felt like I had little to look forward to. Running the business felt like a slog. I wasn't living the life I loved. The sorrow of my nephew's illness, the exhaustion of being mum to a toddler and just life, was all a bit much.

I was talking to my dad and he said, "Oh, do you want to come to Bali with me next month? I'm going to the FAPAA (Federation of Asia Pacific Aircargo Associations) conference."

I replied, "You know what, Dad? You've caught me in a whimsical mood. Sure, let's go."

I ran it by Mathew of course and he said, "If it's going to help you feel better and get your mojo back, go for it." What a darling. Clearly, he was not enjoying my funk any more than I was. I looked up flights and got a good ticket price. I found a hotel I could afford across the road from where dad was staying and said, "Lock it in, Eddie." Five days in Bali was just what I needed. The f*ck-it-all mood lifted. I was back in the zone.

Did I have a lot of spare cash at the time? Nope. And a concerned friend reminded me when I said, "By the way, I'm buggering off to Bali in three weeks." She knew I felt stressed about money and the business. I said, "When is there ever enough money to just bugger off?" So, I spent the money and I went for it. I felt so close to burnout. Getting away and making this time for me to rest, recover and rejuvenate felt like the only option.

One week after booking, I received a big tax refund. It was four times what I invested in the trip. Yes, I use the word "invested." My motto of "rest and receive" had again rung true. And it will ring true for you. When you prioritize rest and back yourself, the universe delivers amazing opportunities and will take care of you. That is my experience. Yes, I am a little woo-woo. But, hey, in my experience, this really works. And I've shared many examples throughout this book.

When you put your rest, leisure, travel and well-being first, you will receive a big payoff.

Those five days re-energized and ignited me in a way I couldn't have imagined. I had ideas again. I was creative again. I wanted to work on my business again. I had that energy to think again. I also met amazing connections because I said yes to joining my dad at the conference. One of those led to a new client and new business in India.

FALL BACK IN LOVE WITH HOME

After spending five days in a tropical location, you'd think coming home would be a downer. Of course, coming home to my boys is never a sad thing. I missed them but, yes, reality can sometimes knock all the travel goodness out of you. If you let it.

The day I arrived home, I went through our apartment front gate and not the garage entrance. Good choice. I was greeted by blue skies, and dappled sunshine on my face as it peeked through the palms. Tropical plants lined the path to my apartment. I turned to the left and saw our swimming pool glistening in the midday sun. It all took my breath away. "This is where I live. I love where I live."

I fell back in love with our apartment, our location and our choice of home area, the Gold Coast. This is my playground, my office and my home. It's Australia's most popular travel destination, and I get to live here. I choose to live here. We put our rental plans to move on hold. We embraced our lovely apartment again, with its stunning outlook and convenient location, gorgeous wildlife and a bevy of activity for families.

We will love this house until we are ready for that next step. And, for us and for now, apartment living suits us perfectly. We can just lock the front door and leave. Well, once we get a pet sitter for our gorgeous fur baby, T'challa. There is no better setup for us to enjoy as much travel as possible in the next few years—domestically and internationally.

If you don't love where you live, move. But consider seeing your home with a traveler's eyes. Can you find some things to love about it?

HOW TO ENJOY A STAYCATION

Here are some tips from an article I wrote for She Defined:

Set yourself a challenge

I challenged myself to go to the beach for 10 minutes every day for seven weeks after realizing I wasn't going much despite bragging about my beachside home whenever I traveled. It was so calming and enjoyable, and it didn't take me long each day—just 10 minutes, though I often stayed longer. What's a simple and fun challenge you can set for yourself near home?

Plan a date night or outing

We plan elaborate and wonderful activities on vacations. But we don't always know the best nearby restaurants and activities at home. Plan a catch-up or date night. Suggest meeting at X place, at X time, to do X. Be specific and make it easy for the other person to say, "Yes."

Go to a famous local tourist spot

How often have you heard yourself say, "Oh that's just a tourist spot?" But have you ever been to it? A visit to an art gallery, museum, popular restaurant, winery or brewery in your own city might be just the thing to make you feel you're on vacation. Why not?

Ask a visitor for tips

Often when I mention where I live to others, within minutes they rattle off activities and locations I've never heard of. Ask a visitor what they love about your city. Where did they go and what did they do?

Places you never thought of visiting could take on a whole new life when seen through the eyes of someone else.

Take a new path

Yes, it can be that simple. During COVID-19, I realized that instead of walking on the sidewalk near the water, I could take off my shoes and walk on the sand and put my feet in the water. It sounds like the stupidest aha moment, but it really was a revelation to me. We get so set in our ways that we cannot see the alternative paths available to us. It took a pandemic for me to realize I could get my daily dose of sun and sand meters from my home.

AVOID THE POST VACATION BLUES

If you are not quite convinced about the staycation and you're longing to travel and explore, here are some tips for how to avoid post-vacation blues.

Always have the next trip planned

I'm not suggesting you enter an endless loop of putting deposits on vacations but have a plan of where you want to go next or something to work toward, as an inspiration through that difficult "settling back in" phase. This is manifesting 101. You dream it, you envision it and then you work toward it to make it a reality. Also, planning is part of the fun.

Embrace the daily grind

I know this might seem like the antithesis to my Bleisure movement message but stay with me. Travel can feel so busy. So many things to see, so many things to do, so many wonderful experiences to enjoy. You feel you must make the most of every moment. And while the Bleisure life allows you to relax about "needing a holiday" and having to make the most of this one trip, it's easy to get caught up in the "must see, must do" culture of travel and that gets tiring. Sometimes it's nice to get into a rhythm and a routine back at home.

Relive your trip through photos and memories

This is one I love doing with my son. I take a lot of photos and videos while traveling to help me remember everything that happens. Finn and I often watch the photo compilations my iPhone makes. It's such a beautiful way to relive our trips together. He asks questions and we talk about what happened. We also get to share our stories with family and friends. We blast away the post-vacation blues replacing them with fond, warm memories.

Be where you are

The best way to not feel the post-vacation blues is to be aware of where you are. My meditation app recently reminded me, "For the next moment, allow yourself to be a human BEING rather than a human DOING. Do nothing. Just be." Whether you are traveling or at home—with friends, family or alone—be present. Live the life you are in. Now.

Questions for reflection

Remember to write your answers. It really helps.

1. How can you see your own home with new eyes?

2. What do you love about travel? How can you find this when you're not doing the big trips?

3. Perhaps you don't love to travel as much as others (cough, my husband) so what do you do for fun, enjoyment, leisure?

4. What does leisure and rest mean to you?

5. List five new places you can visit near your home.

6. List five new cafes or restaurants you'd like to try.

7. List five activities you'd love to try, such as pottery, art class, singing lesson, tennis, sport.

8. List five activities you love doing inside or near your home.

9. List five people to do stuff with at home or near to your home.

See, look at all the amazing ways you can see your local area, your city or even your own country with new eyes. Even better, you can share it with others who want to do the same.

Short and sweet

- Embrace the traveler mindset, even when you're at home.

- See your surroundings with fresh eyes; find joy and wonder in simple things.

- Act like a tourist at home and celebrate your local area. Explore what's on offer as if you were a visitor.

- Ask a visitor what they love about where you live.

- Find adventure in the everyday. Have a curious mind and be as excited about your own country as you are abroad.

- Create a life list. Unlike a bucket list, which is focused on the end of your days, a life list is about doing what you love now while you are young enough to enjoy it.

- Walk a new path. It can be as simple as taking a new route home to see and experience new things.

15

IT'S TIME FOR YOU

My lovely one, we've reached the end, for now. What an adventure we've had together.

And now it's time for you to go out there and live the life of your dreams. Travel the world. See amazing places. Yes, there will be work, there will be sacrifices, but you can have the life you want now.

You don't have to wait until retirement to live. You don't have to rely on your annual leave as the only way to travel and take breaks. You can create an alternative career path. I have shown you multiple ways to work; there is no set way. I have shared the stories of the other beautiful people who have lived a life they love, traveling and working in many ways. Whether you are in a corporate role, a casual job or you run a business, allow yourself to do what you love now.

Remember, you do not have to make travel your work, to become a travel agent, an air steward or a travel writer. Instead, you can do the work you normally do from anywhere in the world. And you don't have to do the volume of travel I do. Absolutely no one, including me, is advocating for that (anymore).

Bleisure means combining business, leisure and travel. To join the Bleisure movement, you must first identify what you enjoy doing. Then do more of that, whether you do it locally, domestically or internationally. Having a traveler mindset means you are always looking at the world in new ways and finding awe and inspiration in simple sights, sounds and activities.

It doesn't have to be all or nothing. Feast or famine. You don't have to save, save, save, then enjoy. You don't have to work, work, work and then play. You can consistently generate income, grow wealth, have stability and still have adventure. It's taken me a long, long time—15 years in business and even longer in my life—to realize this. It is so liberating.

Look at the challenges you have faced in your life. When did life feel harder? How can you take those lessons and do things differently in future? It's not impossible. Of course, sometimes your plans don't work out. As Jodie Fox said at the Business Chicks Movers & Breakers Conference in 2022 about closing her business, Shoes of Prey, "Sometimes you win, sometimes you learn."

GIVE IT A GO

Don't be afraid to try. In 2024, the university where I studied, the University of Technology Sydney, invited me to give a speech on the alternative career path to the university alumni. That speech laid the groundwork for this book. I shared how I'd made money and traveled the world. A member of the audience approached me afterward and said his key takeaway was that I gave things a go. I didn't always know if an idea would work or how it would work, but I gave many ideas a crack.

He had my message in a nutshell, and when he reflected it back to me, I saw it, too. Yes, I've had a go. I've given it a crack. And most of the time, it worked out in the end. If it didn't, I've learned, tweaked my approach and I've adapted.

But I started.

And you, my lovely, must start somewhere. Start today. Don't let your dreams, your goals, and your vision for your life wait any longer. Because the reality is stark: we do not know how long we have in this life.

Do not wait until a major life event shocks you into going after your dreams. You don't need to break your back as I did. You don't need to break your mind. And you don't have to suffer tragedy after tragedy to do what YOU want to be doing.

It's about what you want to do, not what others expect you to do. Even if you don't quite know what you want to do, make a choice and try something. Start today. Choose a path and follow it. See if it is for you. Learn, tweak your approach and adapt.

TAKE BREAKS

And remember, take breaks. Please, lovely one, take a break. Don't physically, mentally or emotionally break before you give yourself permission to take a rest and create time for yourself. Run your business, follow your career, travel the world, have your family, and live a life you love now.

You can do that. I know because I am.

Thank you lovely for being here. Now go out there and start your Bleisure journey today.

Question for reflection

What will you do to start your Bleisure Life Action Plan today?

Short and sweet

Live a life you love now.

IN HONOR

To my nephew Louis Lovell, for reminding us to focus on what we CAN do in whatever time we receive on this earth.

$1 from every book will go to the Bear Cottage, NSW, Australia.

Bear Cottage provides support, respite and end-of-life care for children with life-limiting conditions and their families, in a warm, homelike environment. They support families who are making every moment count and creating lifelong memories with their darling little ones. My family is forever grateful for how they supported my nephew Louis throughout his short life, and ultimately providing a sanctuary for all of us to shower him with love in his final days.

TRIBUTES

To those who are no longer with us, but who I think of often. Thank you for continuing to inspire, motivate and encourage me.

Ben: A brief conversation at a party when we were both 18 will stay with me forever. The sheer perspective and worldview you shared is what I remember. If I am ever in doubt, I think back to our conversation and I know what I must do. Time is short, but we can make the most of it. Thank you.

Rory: Every time I have a challenge, I see you standing there egging me on. If you are doing it, I'll take it on, too. "What would Rory do?" I ask myself. "He'd go for it." Thank you, my friend.

Kerry: Thank you for being the voice of encouragement, even though you're gone. I know you would have been my first reader, and I miss your wise counsel and guidance. Thank you for always being my cheerleader, champion and confidant.

Deb: *Mi buena amiga.* Your time was too short, but I still feel your joy. You took me in and gave me a home in our fabulous Mexico uni days. You shared your space and your heart with me. I am inspired to go after my dreams NOW and not wait for "one day." This is the gift you've left me. *Espero que estés bailando en el cielo. Besos amiga, te echo de menos. Muchas gracias por tus recuerdos.*

Steph: "You light up the world." These were the last words you said to me and the ones that will stay in my heart forever. You lived life to the max and I'm so inspired by the woman, the mother, the friend, the wife and the legend that you were. Memories of your smile still brighten my world.

Grannie: We shared joy, infectious laughter and a passion for travel. You believed in me. You supported me and you encouraged me. You told me I was successful. That meant the world to me and, no matter what, I'll always know that I have achieved success in your eyes and in my own. Thank you for being proud of me. I'll continue to chase after my dreams with you in my heart and mind.

Uncle John: You were an adventurer and always up for new experiences. I love how you backed yourself and built a life here in Australia. I'm grateful for the love and support you gave to my parents when they first arrived in 1981, and how your extended family also became ours. Your home is my heart's home. You've taken me in when I needed space and loved me. You made me go for walks when I was in my head. You taught me the most ridiculous and obscure things and challenged me to think more about the problems I have faced. I miss your laugh, but I feel it in my heart. I'll always be thankful for the times we spent together and how you inspired me to go after my dreams. You and Aunty Joan are the kind of couple I'd like to be. I love how you loved each other. To be in your presence was a joy. You lived life to the max. Thank you. I'll always look to you as a guiding light.

ACKNOWLEDGEMENTS

Dear Reader,

First, thank you for being here, for saying "yes" to my book and for reading my words. It's the greatest honor. This book was a long time in the making. I've read many books over the years that I have been dreaming about writing it. I've seen authors in the past write their book was a long time coming and I thought, "Well, what took you so long?" And then I remember my journey. I knew I would write a book after my gap year in 2007, but I didn't know it would be this book. I thought it would be a how-to travel like I did. And I guess, in a small part, it is. So, thank you for being here now and reading my words.

Acknowledgements doesn't usually get a chapter, but as this was SO long in the making, I wanted to ensure I acknowledged those who have been a part of the journey.

Lydia FillBach: I met you on a dolphin retreat in the Bahamas in 2014, then stayed at your home later that year in Vienna, Austria. You read my human design chart and told me I wasn't creative. I felt devastated and my mind jumped to my book. I told you how deeply I wanted to write a book one day. Was that dream not meant to be? You explained in more detail. I'm more like a journalist, an observer, a storyteller. I don't create things from scratch, like a songwriter or an artist or a poet; I document and observe experiences. But you reassured me. I was just collecting experiences and the book would come. I sure have collected experiences. There's 72,000 words here, and there could have been so many more. I'm glad I wrote this book. Yours was the message I needed to ensure this book got into the world. So, thank you, Lydia.

Anastasia Tsikas: As my accountability buddy from Business Chicks—Business Club, you gave me the assurance that my book would make it into the world—not just one book, but two. So, stay tuned. There are 10 or more book ideas I've written down so far. Ana, you've given me the peace to sit with this idea and capture this knowledge. You told me my book would "drop in" when it needed to. This is the book that came into the world, and I'm so grateful for your sage advice and divine guidance. I appreciate your ongoing support.

Mi amor, my scuba Steve, my very own Aquaman, Mathew: Thank you for your patience, your love and your solid-as-a-rock foundation in my life. I'm a hurricane, a tornado and a lightning bolt of energy. You ground me, help me soar and give me a greater "why." You challenge me more than I'd like some days, and you make me smile. You make me do better and be better. Thank you for the adventurous life and the freedom to pursue my heart's desire. I wouldn't want to do this ride with anyone but you. *Te amo x.*

My dear sweet Finn: You are joy. You are light and you are freedom embodied. Please stay as free and wild as you are and know that mummy will always be your biggest cheerleader, champion and most willing travel buddy. I love you, my darling.

Mumma: You gave me life, so I think you get the biggest thanks of all. And you gave me a beautiful childhood. I always knew how fortunate I was. The choice to come to Australia was the right one and we lived an amazing life because of that decision. You never stopped me or held me back. You knew if you opposed me, I'd just do it anyway to prove you wrong (sorry, ha ha, x). You supported me even when I worried you with my adventures. You never said "don't" or "you can't" when I shared my big dreams. You believe in me. Thank you. It means the world to have your support. Thank you for your help with one of the biggest goals of my life, this book. Reading it, cheering me on, helping me with cover designs and choosing photos. You know me and I trust and appreciate your opinion. Love you, Mumma.

Papa: One of my earliest and most regular travel companions. Twenty countries and counting together. What adventures we've had. I know we are alike and our love for travel connects us. Traveling to the U.S.A. with you and having a four-generations gathering with Cuzzy, you, me and Finn was so precious. Your daring spirit brought you to Australia and gave us so many opportunities. Thank you for being courageous and following your own dream. I'm grateful for your support and guidance in business. Even when I was just nine years old, you encouraged me to pursue my endeavors. I love our business chats, travel dreams and the way you've always supported me to go big. At times you've been worried for my future and stability, but you've backed me and celebrated me. You've been there when I stumbled and helped me to get back on my feet. Love you, Papa x. Here's to many more adventures. And thank you for my cover outfit as an early birthday gift. It's so fab.

To my siblings, James and Andie: Wow we've had some adventures. Our lives have taken us off in different directions but I treasure the times we come together as a trio. Getting to have these shared memories, and having people who know me as I truly am, is a bond like no other. I know it's not always easy having a sister who needs her own GPS tracker, but I appreciate your encouragement and support. And some of our earliest family holidays, Bali and the U.K. to U.S.A. trip, are still some of my favorite travel memories of all time. Love you.

Aunty Joan: What would I do without your counsel? When I'm up late, I hear your voice in my head telling me to rest. "Emma dear, go to bed." You are the matriarch of your family and, although we are not related by blood, you embraced me and loved me as your own. I have always felt so supported by you and seen for who I am. I love our conversations, your straight-down-the-line advice and your joyful chuckle. I hope you speed read through this in a matter of days. I can't wait to hear your thoughts. I know I've worried you with such anecdotes in the past. You always assured me I'd be all right and that if all else fails and I end up destitute I can come to you. Your faith gave me strength. Thank you.

Cuzzy Bill: You are the absolute role model in living a life you love and giving me #goals. If you can live to 101 years of age, I can too. But most importantly, you showed me that magic exists and it exists in people. It exists in you. Thank you for sharing your magic with me. I love you always and forever.

Suzie Plush: As my psychologist for 14 years, we've been on a unique journey. Can you believe this? I'm forever grateful for your wisdom, your calming presence, and your ability to guide me through some of the darkest hours of my life. You are an incredible professional and remarkable at what you do, and an unwavering supporter and cheer-leader. Your faith in my ability and interest in my path means so much to me. I cannot express my thanks for the impact you've had in my life. I am so grateful to have had you on the journey so far. Thank you.

To my in-laws, Margaret and Bruce: Thank you for your love and support. You are wonderful grandparents, and I know you love Finn endlessly. By caring for him many times over these past three years, you have allowed me to focus on my work, travel, and enjoy time alone to be me, and to rest and recover when needed. And to write this book. I know he feels loved and cared for when he is with you. He is at ease with you, so I can also be confident and go after my dreams. Thank you for raising the most incredible man, my darling husband, Mathew. I have thanked you in person and I thank you in my heart often. He is a good man and I know that's thanks to you, and his upbringing and the values you instilled in him. I've joined a wonderful family and I'm forever grateful. I love you.

Lou Acheson: You have given me so many opportunities and were one of the earliest people who held me to account for this book. With your regular check-ins over the years, you held the dream for me. That meant so much. Thank you, my colleague and friend.

Kath Walters, my editor: What a dream you are. I am so grateful for the care, consideration and dedication you have given this book. Your sage advice and thoughtful comments throughout the editing made what I thought would be a daunting and challenging process into a delightful experience. With my whole heart, thank you for making this book better.

Michael Hanrahan and the team at Publish Central, my publishers: What a team! Jumping in at the eleventh hour and making this book the best it can be. I'm so grateful for your vast industry experience and helpful guidance.

Erin Huckle, my publicist: You always had the job. You were the only choice. Your wisdom, skill and unwavering support are so appreciated. You light up the room with your smile and I'm so thankful to have you in my corner.

Liv Muir, my brand strategist: I can't believe I thought I'd do this without revamping my brand and you were the only choice. You see me as I am and it's thanks to you and that fateful dinner (you know the one) that I found alignment with the Bleisure life. Thank you for your work, guidance, patience and kindness. You help me be ME.

Leith Hudson, graphic designer: Thank you for my epic book cover. I'm so happy that we could make a dream come true together: me writing a book and you designing a cover. And for the visual design of so much of my brand: stunning.

Jade Warne, photographer, content creator and biz bestie: I could write a novel on our friendship and working relationship. You were the only choice for the cover photo and, as always, you delivered way above and beyond. You help me shine and I'm forever thankful. Be the rose, my friend.

Lesley Chambers, audiobook producer and chief cheerleader: How blessed I am to have you as a client, supplier and friend. Showing up at my UTS talk and cheering me on; I will never forget. You helped me grow and develop my business as my ideal client. And now you've shared your exceptional expertise with producing my audiobook. Thank you.

Holly Rose, makeup artist: You make me look incredible. I will pack you in my suitcase one day and take you wherever I go. Thank you for your artistry but also for being an incredible champion and support for this very special book cover shoot.

Lyn Taylor, desk and studio: Thank you for your beautiful space and the fun we've had working in it over the past few years. And for being there on my most important photoshoot to date, this book cover photo, to capture all the behind-the-scenes action and to lift me up.

Amber Field, executive assistant: You are so much more than an EA. You are a gift. How will I ever function again without you? Don't leave me, please. Thank you for your patience, initiative, kindness and mum-ness. You force me to stop, switch off and go to bed. We all need an Amber in our lives. You can have her a little but save some for me.

Dan Cutamora and Maureen Comeo, my virtual assistants: You make me look good. I'm so grateful to have you on my team. Let's continue to grow and learn together. And so excited for the company retreat. Next stop, Philippines.

To my early readers: Lizzie McCauley, Erin Huckle, Kate Merryweather, Sally Branson, Annette Densham, Hannah Wood, Amanda Ewin, Shari Brewer, Jana Newman and Angela Pickett. You jumped in when I needed you most to be an extra pair of eyes and some wise counsel. Thank you.

Kate Toon: Thank you for doing business your way and showing me how fast an author can get a book to market. I was like, "Game on." Thanks for showing me the way. And thank you for being bold and sliding into my direct messages to ask me, "Really. How do you travel so much?" It helped me realize that running my business and traveling the world is a unique skill, and I can help people to do the same. Your question sparked my new business direction and the concept for my first ever book. Forever thankful.

Emma Isaacs: Thank you for being you. Thank you for such an incredible venue for my book launch. Thank you for the kind and brilliant words in the foreword of this book. You inspired me with your book *Winging It: Stop Thinking, Start Doing*, and your dream of a big life. Your bravery has pushed me to aim higher and achieve more. Thank you, my friend.

To all the beautiful Business Chicks: I love you all, and there's too many of you to name. Being part of your community has helped me grow as a businesswoman, a mother, and as a human these past four years, and I'm grateful for the endless love and support I get. Together, we do great things.

To the University of Technology Sydney alumni and my contact Theresa Winters: As I have said, talking about my alternate career path to the alumni in March 2024 laid the foundation of this book. I wrote 12,000 words to prepare for that talk; many ended up in what you're reading here today. It was a full circle moment to go back to my university, the place where my business began 14.5 years ago. It was an honor and a privilege and confirmed I was on the right path. It's the book I wish I'd had when I was finishing university. I wish someone had told me I could choose the alternate path where I could have a business and a child and a house and choose to live a life that I love. I did it anyway (I love a challenge), but it would have helped to have some tips. To the people I met there, to anyone who's just finishing university or who's in that sort of first midlife crisis in your late 20s—it's OK to be you. It's OK to do what you want. It's OK to give things a shot and to figure it out as you go. I have.

To all my clients: Thank you for your support and for choosing my business these past 15 years. I am so grateful for your loyalty, trust, and for the lessons we've learned along the way. It is my honor to serve you, and I'm so grateful for the life you've helped me build.

As much as I wish to thank everyone who has touched my life in these past 15 years of business, I cannot. Let alone the 37 years of my existence and all the people who have touched my life and changed me, whether it be positively or by challenging me to grow. There aren't enough pages. Know that I think of you and I thank you. I am who I am because of all of it and I don't regret a thing. My deepest gratitude to you all. This book wouldn't be what it is without those colorful experiences and I continue to learn and grow because of it all.

So, if you're reading this, and you know who you are and how you've supported my journey, please give yourself a hug and know that I'm grateful to you. We can't do this alone and I wouldn't be here without my business and life village.

OK. I'll save some thankyous for the next book.

But for now, thank YOU for getting to this last line. Without readers, there would be no books. Thank you for choosing me and mine.

Now go out there and live a life YOU love.

Work with me

ONLINE COURSE:
THE BLEISURE LIFE PLAN

Ready to start living a life you love now?

Want the step-by-step plan to incorporate
more Bleisure into your life?

Stay tuned for The Bleisure Life Plan,
a self-paced online course.

Coming soon. Register here.

SPEAKER AND EMCEE

Book me for your next event

I'm a passionate, professional and "Lovell-y" speaker who can help your audience let go of fear and embrace the Bleisure life.

I bring energy, enthusiasm and expertise to travel, leadership and membership events, inspiring and motivating everyone to discover a world of freedom and choice.

When emceeing, I help the guests shine. When speaking, I offer value and guidance that uplifts and empowers.

Whether it's an intimate room, a big conference or the virtual stage, I love engaging with audiences and showing them how to integrate travel and work seamlessly.

Let's inspire your audience to live a life they love.

Signature talks on the Bleisure life, culture and experiences

- **Redefining Travel:** Beyond Holidays: Integrating Travel into Your Daily Life and Business.
- **Alternative Career Paths:** Breaking Free from the 9-5: Building a Flexible Career around Travel.
- **Bleisure Lifestyle:** The Art of Bleisure: Balancing Business, Travel and Self-Care.
- **Travel as Self-Care:** Using Travel as a Tool for Mental Health, Avoiding Burnout and Building Personal Growth.
- **The Bleisure Culture:** Retain Your Best Staff—Create a Bleisure Culture.

Don't see quite what you want? Let's chat about what you're looking for.

EXPERIENCE A TRANSFORMATIONAL RETREAT

My retreats offer you the perfect opportunity to make amazing new friends and connections while nurturing yourself, shedding the expectations of the everyday and opening yourself up to what's possible.

Embrace the Bleisure lifestyle and join us on a transformative journey.

Explore my next retreats.

YOU CAN RUN PROFITABLE RETREATS

Presented as a MINI retreat at a luxurious destination for one day of inspiration, planning and action

Calling all yoga and wellness practitioners, authors, coaches and community hosts.

Are you ready to take your business to the next level? Discover the secrets to creating transformative and profitable retreat experiences during this full-day program.

I guide you in creating transformative experiences that are both fulfilling for your clients and financially viable for you. With my guidance, you'll learn to navigate the complexities of the retreat industry, ensure attendee satisfaction and achieve business success.

Ready to dive into the world of retreats?

Let's create something extraordinary together.

Join me on this journey to mastering the art of retreats, where we transform spaces, lives and futures.

CORPORATE TRAINER AND CONSULTANT

Keep your workforce engaged with a Bleisure culture

I'm sure I don't have to remind you—silent resignation is real.

When your employees show up physically but are checked out mentally, their productivity and engagement sink and take your business with it.

The fact you're here tells me you value your employees' engagement and enjoyment.

But you might not have thought about blending business and leisure to foster a more engaged and motivated workforce. Or know how to do it successfully.

That's where I come in.

As a corporate consultant and trainer, I can activate frameworks, systems, and approaches to integrate Bleisure into your corporate culture.

Let's chat about boosting your business culture. Contact me.

PRIVATE COACHING

Design Your Dream Life

Feeling trapped and burnt out is no way to live your life.

You deserve more than just going through the motions every day.

So many people look at me and think, *I wish I could do that.*
Well, I'm here to help you do exactly that.

In just 60 minutes of 1:1 coaching, you can find the clarity
and direction you need to break free from the work hard,
play hard cycle and start living the Bleisure Life.

Investment:

- $495 for a single session
- $1250 for three sessions used within three months

Book Now

And ... coming soon

The Art of Retreats: Travel the world while running profitable and transformative retreats

THE ART OF
RETREATS

Travel the world
while running profitable and
transformative retreats

EMMA LOVELL

Yes, my next book. Coming in 2025.

Let's play a game

Thank you again for reading all the way to the end. I would love to see this book travel the world. We're starting a Bleisure movement. So, I've got some fun ways you can help me and keep paying it forward.

1. Snap a photo of the book or you with the book on your travels in different countries around the world and tag it #TheArtofBleisure and #BleisureLife. You can also tag me on Instagram, @emmalovell.au

2. Recommend this book to people you know in foreign countries. The more the better. My goal is to visit every member country of the United Nations around the world, but I want to see if my book can get there before I can. I'll be keeping a record.

3. Finished with the book? That's great. Leave it on a plane, train or bus. Pop it on the shelf of a hotel or hostel library. Put it in a community or street library. I'd love to see this book paid forward to fellow travelers. Write a cute message in it and don't forget to use the library card on the page so others can see where it's traveling to. Let's see how far one copy can go. If you do, don't forget to take a photo and share the #TheArtofBleisure and #BleisureLife so I can keep up with its adventures too.

4. Loved the book and want to keep it? That fills me with joy and I am so grateful. How about buying a second copy and gifting it to a friend, family member or colleague who could use a bit more Bleisure in their life too? I would love that.

Thank you again, and I can't wait to hear about your Bleisure life. Email me at emma@emmalovell.au with Bleisure Life in the title and let me know how you've supported the Bleisure movement.

BLEISURE BOOK CARD

DATE	NAME	CITY, COUNTRY	MESSAGE FOR NEXT READER
21/08/24	LOVELLY (EMMA)	GOLD COAST, AUSTRALIA	LIVE A LIFE YOU LOVE